The Church That Heals

The Church That Heals

Simple Strategies for Cultivating Emotional Safety in Your Ministry

Breanna M. Spriggs, LPC-S

Foreword by: Pastor Lucretia R. Church

Published by: Breanna M. Spriggs, LPC-S

CONTENTS

CONTENTS

Paperback: 979-8-9885594-0-5
Ebook: 979-8-9885594-1-2
Library of Congress Control Number: 2023912264
First paperback edition 2023.

Edited by Gina Mushynysky
Cover art by Roger Raymond
City of Publication: Lafayette, La

Printed by IngramSpark in LaVergne, Tennessee.
IngramSpark.com

To my mom:
Thanks for the search that you went on to find Christ. It led us not only to church but also into the life that God intended for us to have. Your search gave our whole family a new legacy in Christ. To the best of your ability, you stood on the Word of God and continually passed your devotion down to us. Let this book be the evidence of all of the seeds that you planted and the outcome of the "yes" that you gave to God back in 1993.

To Bro. Roge':
Thanks for the example that you brought into our lives and set, as a man of God and teacher of His Word. Thanks for modeling and teaching me faithfulness to the house and things of God. Thanks for allowing me the space to ask questions, explore thoughts, and challenge traditions. You have always welcomed me into the conversation, and this book is the evidence of that.

To Ms. Rose:
You have been a destiny helper to me, as well as a second mom. You told me when God told you that I needed to write this book, and you never stopped encouraging me to do so. The calls and the question "How many pages do you have?" held me accountable to

the commission that God gave to me. Thanks for the fuel and love to see it all the way through.

To Pastor Donnie Bolden Sr. and my Lighthouse for Jesus family:
Thank you for being the church community that helped to heal a single mother and her two children back in 1993. Through you all I gained a community and another family. You have always had my back and celebrated the woman that God was making me into. From playing bass to rapping to ministering the Word of God, you all have always been a solid foundation for me to grow on. The examples that you set, the standard that you raised, and the love that you extended still flows through my heart today.

To Prophetess Anna Bolden:
I wish that you were here to see this. You carried a presence of healing. It poured out in your words. We were engulfed in it with your hugs, and we saw it in how you fulfilled your ministry on this earth. I feel so blessed to have encountered you in this lifetime. Hopefully, we will chat about this in the next one.

To Brandon:
Throughout this process, you have been such an encourager and purpose pusher. Even in times when I may have grown weary with the process, you would make sure to give me a nudge and remind me how much the world needs what I have. The journey of our family has been one of healing, and as I always say, I would not want to be on this journey with anyone else but you . . . and the Zeekster, of course!

To the Church:
You saved my life and introduced me to who I was always created to be. I am forever grateful for the love, support, and fellowship that I have been privileged to gain through you. Many have come to doubt your significance in the earth in these times. However, I see you as the hidden treasure that all will come to find refuge in. I hope that this book plays a part in highlighting the latter glory that you will embody within these times. "The glory of this latter house shall be greater than of the former, saith the Lord of hosts: and in this place will I give peace, saith the Lord of hosts" (Haggai 2:9).

Is your church a safe place? Are you and your staff safe places for all kinds of people, including the wounded, recovering, or "unsure of what is wrong with them" kinds of people? Isaiah 53:5 foretells that through the lashes Jesus took on His body, people would be healed. Is your church a safe place where Jesus pours oil on heart wounds to make well the "I need healing, can you help me?" kinds of people? Most leaders would answer with an emphatic "Yes, we are a very healthy church." However, some may bravely admit that they are not quite sure and wish there was a way to take their church's proverbial temperature.

If you are one of the latter, there is good news. *The Church That Heals* is one of the greatest resources, given by God in this generation, for the health of the church and surrounding communities. Written by Breanna Spriggs, LPC-S, it offers years of personal wisdom and professional expertise in a one-of-a-kind workbook format. Breanna's style of teaching is Spirit-led, spirited, practical, humorous, and professional. She has helped bring hundreds, if not thousands, of people to wellness. The title of the workbook alone gives a glimpse into her heart as a mental health professional and citizen of heaven who wants to see each member of the church functioning at their optimal self.

Through *The Church That Heals* you may realize possible leanings, religious or otherwise, toward ministering to those with mental health issues. The workbook will challenge or solidify structures in your belief systems and give you tools to identify and assist those struggling with mental illness, mental health, psychological challenges, or deep hurts. It will provide information to best serve the people God has entrusted you with. Neither you nor the members of your congregation will any longer have to feel powerless against the giant called mental health.

Finally, this workbook will help you understand the importance of sharing the load of service with those who co-labor with you in God's work. It will assist you in recognizing and making full use of their gifts and other resources in your community, possibly protecting you and your staff's mental wellness. Sometimes knowing who to direct someone to for help is half the battle. If you are interested in this invaluable resource, then grab your pen; gather your staff and ministry workers. This workbook is about to equip each one of you to be a safe place known as *The Church That Heals*.

—Evangelist Lucretia Church
www.lucretiachurch.com

INTRODUCTION

Mental health has been a taboo subject within the context of the church for a long time. The mental health of those within the church has been even more taboo. Our beliefs generally nudge us into the lane of taking those things to God and assuming that somehow He will cause them to "magically," or spiritually, go away. There's only one problem: they don't. No matter how much we pray, shout, preach, etc., the human soul still feels, and those feelings cannot be anesthetized by a good church service and age-old colloquialisms. Many people are becoming more aware of their pain, and the first place that they run to is the church—as they should.

The purpose of this book is to provide church leaders and members with a tool that will guide us in providing support to those individuals who come to the church for help. *The Church That Heals* provides the basic knowledge of how to support and guide an individual to safety in what may be the lowest moment of their life. In doing so, this book also increases the confidence of the church in general in its ability to minister effectively to mental health issues and to direct individuals in need to appropriate resources within the community.

Ultimately, through this book, I hope to reconnect the institution of the church with the people in the church. When Jesus healed, He was moved by His own compassion. Jesus did not only see people,

He saw needs—and He was always equipped to meet those needs. I would also like to do my part in restoring the emotional health of the church. By not being able to properly attend to emotional and mental health needs in the church, we compromise the health of the church. If our people are not healthy and our methods are not healthy, then we, as the church, are not healthy. If we continue in unhealthy patterns, we risk misrepresenting the holiness of God that we are to reflect to others.

I also hope to support the church in becoming a safer place for all who God draws through its doors. Many people, often from all walks of life, come into the church. The church should possess an inherent gentleness and sensitivity to the pain that these individuals may carry. Gentleness is a fruit of the Spirit (Galatians 5:22); therefore, if the Spirit is in our church, then gentleness should abide there as well. Individuals should know that their story, their experience, and their brokenness are safe within the walls of the church and with its people. We should be able to be vulnerable within the body of Christ. However, for years that has not been our primary reputation. Church has become the place where we must bring our best, most righteous selves; and because of that, we learn to spiritually soar as we emotionally fade . . . one service at a time.

In effort to paint a picture of the need, lifewayresearch.com reports that only 27 percent of churches have a plan to assist families affected by a mental illness and 49 percent of pastors say they rarely or never speak to their congregation about mental illness. The site also reports that 65 percent of churchgoing family members of those with mental illness want their church to talk openly about mental illness.[1] Further, the site indicates that 80 percent of pastors said that their church is equipped to assist someone who is threatening to take their own life, but only 47 percent of churchgoers who had lost a loved one to suicide reported that their church leaders were aware of their loved one's struggles.

Quite a few years ago, I was deeply affected when a prominent figure in my church community attempted to take their own life. I often wondered how we had missed the signs. Had this person reached out to anyone? If so, what were they told? Could they simply have been encouraged to pray about it? What shook me to the core was that there was not much conversation about it afterward. The person and everyone around them just continued forward. I never knew if that was a good or bad thing (it may be a little bit of both).

Third John 1:2 expresses a wish that we would all prosper and be in good health, even as our soul (which is our mind, will, and emotions) prospers. This verse shows biblically that God values our health and wellness. Jesus's ministry touched every part of our humanity through His own humanity. In Scriptures like Luke 3:11, He promoted care. We see illustrations of Jesus weeping, feeling abandoned, and even enduring trauma. Why? Because if He was to be fully man, He had to. Unfortunately, being human comes with fears, abandonment, and trauma. Jesus was willing to feel exactly what we sometimes feel in our lives. Hebrews 4:15 illustrates this, contrasting Jesus with high priests who cannot be touched with the feelings of our infirmities. The Bible paints a picture of Jesus as the God who "gets it." If we, the church, are His hands and feet, how much more should we seek to be people (of God) who get it?

In Revelation 3:17, we see the church of Laodicea being scolded for being unaware of their own brokenness. Why was this a problem? First, they were not existing in the truth. We cannot worship God "in spirit and in truth" (John 4:24) by hiding the broken parts of ourselves from Him. Believe it or not, true worship requires vulnerability. Second, if we do not show our own brokenness, then our healing becomes superficial. This may cause those who are broken among us to feel that their pain is out of Jesus's reach. Little do they know that we all house the same pain. In church, it is common to hear people speak of us singing a song that "the angels cannot sing." I believe that this song is a song of His redemption, healing, and restoration. However, we must live in the light of truth in order to sing that song.

This book is meant to be an interactive training workbook. At the end of each chapter are endnotes that will contain additional information, commentary and references. Read them, as you progress through the chapters, in order to gain more insight and background information. Throughout the process of reading the book, you will also be prompted to look within and examine where you are, as you consider the concepts that are presented.

Exercise

Let's start now by simply examining the mindsets and misconceptions that you have or may have encountered about mental health and the church. Write the first three that come to mind.

1. _____

2. _____

3. _____

I hope that you wrote things like "Depression can be prayed away, and if prayer alone does not work, then the person lacks faith." I challenge you to keep these mindsets and misconceptions at the forefront of your mind as you read this book. It is those mindsets that may cause you to feel uncomfortable as you read, and it is those mindsets that causes others to feel uncomfortable with seeking help from the church and those in the church, as well. I hope that by the end of this book, you will have a renewed perspective about how an equipped church, believer, or minister can change the course of a person's mental and emotional battles.

This book is organized into three parts: Connect, Serve, and Construct. These are the three umbrellas that all things "safety and the church" fall under. The Connect section addresses the internal work that each individual or team will need to do in order to create and maintain an atmosphere that is conducive to providing support. The Serve section provides each individual or team with practical tools with which they will be able to approach common needs/ problems that they could potentially be presented with within the church. The Construct section provides a road map for moving forward to construct a system that is equipped to consistently maintain the use of the processes and tools that are outlined in this book.

How This Book May Be Used

The Church That Heals may be used by individual Christians who would like to become more understanding of and helpful to fellow Christians who may need support from them at any time. Many times, we find ourselves blindsided by cries for help from those around us. The tools in this book will provide you with basic skills to be able to walk alongside those in pain or at the very least, to be able to distinguish when you may not be the right person to walk a person through their current pain. Oftentimes, the best help that you can give a person is to point them in the direction of someone who is better equipped to help them. Ultimately, the purpose of this book is to provide the tools to remove the risk of harm from within us and ultimately from within the church.

This book may also be used in small-group settings. In small groups, this book may foster conversations about how we can shift the culture of our churches to be safer. Small groups give the opportunity for conversations to happen from both the perspectives of those who need and give support. A simple conversation may be the catalyst for a major change.

Finally, this book may be used as a leadership training tool to help strengthen church staff and leaders in the area of recognizing and addressing many of the emotional needs that walk through the church doors. This, in turn, will transform the church into a hub of safety and, by the Spirit of Christ, that "strong tower" of Proverbs 18:10. By simply shifting our perspective and increasing our awareness, we, the church, can become closer to God's design. God designed His church to be the safe place to which all may run when they are weary, tired, and in need. As we become a safe place, we will see healing break forth like never before!

INTRODUCTION ENDNOTES

1. This is where our connection to the people matters.

CONNECT

"And I am no longer in the world, but they are in the world, and I am coming to you. Holy Father, keep them in your name, which you have given me, that they may be one, even as we are one." John 17: 11 ESV

1

Be a Safe Place

What does it even mean to be safe place? How can we tell when we are unsafe? The simplest answer to these questions is "by your fruit." In Matthew 7:20, Jesus compares disciples to trees, saying that you can clearly identify what manner of tree a tree is by the fruit that it yields. In Matthew 12:33, He goes further to say that the nature of a tree's fruit is directly related to the nature of the tree. That being said, the first way to know whether you or your church is safe is simply to observe those who are in your atmosphere or culture the most.

As individuals, we should observe the condition of our family, friends, and other Christians when they are in our presence; as a church, we should observe the condition of the families and individuals who are consistently within our fellowships. Are they better or worse because of it? Do you observe genuine smiles and eyes with light behind them? Do you observe people who feel comfortable with sharing honestly, when they do not have a smile to give? Or do you observe heavy, broken, yet silent people? Do you see forced smiles that fade as individuals continue past the superficial "how are yous"? These are the difficult, yet honest, questions that we must ask ourselves as we examine whether we are a safe place for others.

Let's define the word "safe." In this book, I will define safe as simply the state of being absent of the risk of harm: emotionally, spiritually, physically and sexually. Now, I know that there are two types of people reading this book. One type is thinking, "According to that definition, I'm pretty safe." The other type is overwhelmed and thinking, "How can I ever be safe?!" The truth is that the best way to be safe is to be aware (but not overwhelmed and in fear) of the ways that we may be unsafe. So, whether you are a person who feels that you are safe or a person who is overwhelmed at the thought of being unsafe, you can benefit from this rule of thumb: "The road to safety is paved with carefulness."

We are all human, and we truly have no clue about how fragile another person may be. Something so simple as a brash tone can make you unsafe to someone who has endured verbal abuse. Awareness of your tone and mindfulness to speak more softly immediately makes you a safer person. The willingness of each of us to look within and challenge aspects of ourselves that may be harmful to others immediately helps the church, as a whole, to be a safer place. What has made us harmful up to this point has been, unfortunately, our lack of awareness. We have been on autopilot for so long, employing the same ways of being, that we have not realized that the church has become more associated with "church hurt" than with healing. That is a problem.

We are going to unpack ways to become more aware of and connected to our own condition, as well as the condition of those around us, and the barriers to doing so. However, I first want to make the distinction between being unsafe and being abusive. I must first point out that if any form of abuse is happening within your church establishment, you must take immediate and legal action to address those incidents. Oftentimes, within the church setting, people are indirectly harmed because they witnessed abuse that was excused and covered in a church, where they should be able to feel safe. Jesus left the ninety-nine to restore one lost sheep, but He never exposed the ninety-nine to harm by trying to reform a wolf in sheep's clothing. On the other hand, just because an action is not abusive and is accepted does not mean that it is not harmful. These are the actions and behaviors that we will be placing in the hot seat as we continue.

Exercise

If you were to closely and honestly examine yourself, what are some ways in which you may be unsafe to those around you if you are not careful? List them.

1. _____

2. _____

3. _____

Thank you for taking the time to consider and identify that about yourself. I am fully aware that self-examination is difficult. If you were not able to think of anything right away, take time to pray and ask God to reveal those things to you. My core belief is that if you are reading this book, you do not want to continue in any manner that may be harmful to your fellow brothers and sisters in Christ.

As we become more of a safe place for others and become more self-aware of how we may be harmful, establishing rapport with those around us is the next necessary step. The Bible even tells us to "know them which labor among you."[2] We can never know everything that a person has been through or is going through at that moment, but we can be open to getting to know each other and learning others' stories.

Establishing rapport helps us to trust each other and connect to each other past the superficial surface. In order to establish rapport, we must make ourselves available to people. Instead of running straight to your car after church, linger for a moment and introduce yourself to the family that is visiting the church for the first time. Have a conversation with that member of the youth group who started just started high school this year. Just because you have seen that child every Sunday since they were in diapers does not mean that you have a rapport with them. There is no ministry without relationship, and we can never build relationships without establishing a basic rapport with each other.

In addition to making ourselves more available, we also establish rapport through simply showing interest in others. We know that church members sometimes have the reputation of being too nosey, but showing interest in a healthy manner communicates to people that they are seen and important. A major part of being safe is eradicating gossip, which is extremely harmful. Asking a simple question, without probing,[3] can open the door for more rapport-building later. For example, when you approach that new family visiting your church, simply say, "It was good to have you in service today. Is your family new to town as well?" The person may give a simple answer or a detailed answer, depending on many factors, but they will walk away from the conversation feeling noticed.

Another key to building rapport is remembering small details about others. Remembering someone's name or the fact that they asked that their grandmother be placed on the prayer list can go a long way. How would you feel if you were in a new church and one of the ministers passed by you and asked, "How is your grandmother? Our prayer team is still praying for her every Wednesday"? Two seconds' worth of words can make a lasting impact on a person and, ultimately, how safe they feel in the church. The fact that this person is not too busy or important to stop and tell them that they remember your grandmother communicates to you that "you matter here." Where a person feels valued, they are more likely to feel safer.

The next way to be safer is to intentionally *lead* with love. Everything that we do must first be done in love. Love is what identifies us as disciples of Christ. The fact that Jesus said that the world will know who we are by how we love each other shows us how essential love is to being safe. The truth is that it can be easy to love people with whom we are unfamiliar. The more we get to know each other, the more familiar we become with each other's flaws, and suddenly love requires more patience and forbearance. Jesus knew this. He also knew that if He could get twelve guys with totally different personalities and approaches to love each other, they would have no problem loving the world.

Familiarity and treating each other commonly can be something that creeps up on us as our years within a church community add up. We can get to a place where rapport can be more of a hindrance to leading with love than a help. We can reach the place where "I know you so well and you know me so well that carefulness is unnecessary." In cases like this, our relationships within the church are on autopilot, we fade back into unawareness of how we affect each other, the love grows cold, and we ultimately become unsafe to the people with whom we have been in community for years.[4] Leading with love must be an intentional way of being with everyone we encounter, not just newcomers. We tend to take each other for granted, and any time we do that, we increase our risk of harm to each other.

What is love? It is a sense of benevolence or goodwill toward others. First Corinthians 13:4–7 describes that love is kind, thinks no evil, is not easily provoked, and keeps a mindset of hope toward others. When we test our way of being toward each other, does it match this description? Remember that love is not a feeling. It can be expressed through actions, but it is not even actions. In this Scripture, love is described to us as a way of being: a nature. Leading with love means that love is who you are toward all others. Holding ourselves to this standard makes us safe.

Being a safe place is definitely not for the faint of heart. It takes work. It takes being willing to face the barriers that keep us from being safe. This process can be ugly, because it requires us to face ugly truths that we often spend a lot of time trying to avoid or explain away. We will discuss the same barriers, but on three different levels: personal, interpersonal, and structural. You will also be prompted to consider some barriers that may be personally unique to you or the church community that you are in.

The first barrier is old patterns. From the time that we are children, we are groomed into ways of operating based upon the environment we are in. Those patterns (for the most part) helped us to navigate successfully in those spaces. Consequently, what happens as we get older is that we take those patterns and ways of operating into other environments, and those patterns prove to be counterproductive. Changing those patterns requires us to understand that *operating in the ways that kept me safe as a child could be causing me to be unsafe for others in my adulthood.*[5] For example, those who grew up with a reactive parent learn, by default, to manipulate. Such people learned to read that parent's mood in order to know when it is safe to present a need (or any information at all) and avoid that parent's wrath. Eventually, they may learn how to manage that parent's mood through flattery and other methods.[6] That way of operating was necessary to maintain a sense of safety in that environment at that time. Others may have learned other ways of operating that helped them to be safe in their respective environments.

How would this show up interpersonally? Imagine bringing this same way of operating into the church[7] and being a person who uses flattery and "buttering up" to get people to do things and respond in ways that you want them to. In essence, you would be limiting the range of everyone's feelings around you in order for you to feel safer and manipulating situations in order to control the outcomes to be in your favor. In order to change this pattern, you would need to recognize it and understand how it could be harmful to others. This shows up in so many other ways—especially in churches. People-pleasers interact with intimidators, who interact with manipulators, who are trying to interact with isolators . . . and we are all in a power struggle for our own sense of safety.

Structurally, we make up the church. Therefore, the same individuals who struggle with these unsafe patterns of interactions are the pastors, the deacons, the secretaries, the worship leaders, the youth leaders, etc. These ways of operating influence the culture of the whole church. If you, the pastor, are intimidating, then that trait will be expressed through the nature of your teachings and, consequently, reflected in those in the congregation who follow your teachings. It's inevitable. We must hold ourselves accountable to look inward and change unhealthy patterns that are negatively influencing the climate of our church communities.

The next barrier is the lack of intention and not making being safe a priority. On the personal level, one must feel safe, in order to be safe. We are most unsafe, when we are on the defense. It is so important that we learn to examine our own levels of vulnerability at different times and what influences the changes. In order to do this, I must make being safe a priority.

Interpersonally, we must prioritize interacting with others in a safe way. We must consider how we talk to each other, how we listen to each other, and how we regard and respect each other's boundaries. In the structure of the church, we cannot confuse being close-knit with having unhealthy boundaries. Without prioritizing safety, the idea of boundaries becomes a fleeting notion that we only talk about and never actually operate in.

By default, we are who we are, and we bring who we are into every environment: you bring you with you everywhere you go. We must be mindful that the more involved we are in a church community, the more we will influence the culture of how that community operates. If the leadership[8] of a church lends to gossip (which crosses the boundary of privacy), then the leaders' attitude toward gossip can easily permeate the culture of the culture of the church and everyone connected to that leadership team, and communicate to everyone that this is not a safe place to be authentic in. We must prioritize intentionally developing a set of values that will promote both feeling and being safe. If being safe is at the bottom of the totem pole, then we will never address it and overcome unhealthy patterns.

The last barrier that we will highlight is fear. The Bible says that there is no fear in love and that perfect love casts out fear (1 John 4:18). Therefore, if love is our key to being safe, then fear is our kryptonite. Personally, it is impossible to be vulnerable and safe without facing and processing through our fears. Now I know that it is the tendency of many of the saints who are reading this book to get "super spiritual" at this point. We know that God did not give us a spirit of fear and that you can command fear to go in the name of

Jesus, but the truth is that there is a difference between the spirit of fear and feelings of fear.

The spirit of fear points to an inability to trust God to be God and making the choice to live in that space, allowing that fear to be at the core of who you are in life and in your walk with Him. Feeling and experiencing fear is a part of our human experience that must be noticed and managed. Why? Because when we are in fear, we are wired to defend ourselves and everyone is an enemy.

Interpersonally, this is a recipe for disaster, especially if you are in ministry. Interacting with others while entertaining the thought that they could hurt you or take advantage of you will bring up the walls of Jericho in your relationships. Fear will cause you to see everyone as a threat and interact with them as such. Honestly, if I could, I would attribute most of the strife and contention that happens between believers to fear. The pattern goes like this: we fear, we defend, we fight to kill. I do not want to go too far into how we approach political, moral, and scriptural debates, but I am sure that you can do the math.

How does this look on the grand scale? We fear that other Christians—especially those who look different and believe differently—will contaminate us, so we never fellowship with each other. We fear that the new pastor in town will "take our members," so we make negative comments about them to those members. We use hell to instill fear in our kids and manage their behavior instead of actively walking with them through struggles. All of this makes us extremely unsafe. Being in church becomes more about soothing each other's fear of having our feelings hurt and egos bruised than it is about actually being healed and growing closer to God (safely) in the company of other believers. Without addressing this head-on, we risk the church being more known for injury than refuge.

Let's take a deeper look into how this may play out in real time for you.

Exercises

What are some of the patterns that you fall into when you feel unsafe? How does this show up in your interpersonal interactions?

_____

_____

_____

_____

_____

Where have you seen fear play a role in unhealthy patterns in the church community? What would be some ways to face those fears individually or as a community?

_____

_____

_____

_____

_____

Chapter 1 Endnotes

2. First Thessalonians 5:12. (I hope you have your Bible near as you read this book.)

3. A probing question is one that seeks to dig for more information. While building rapport, probing could make someone uncomfortable. Simply thank the person for the information that they do give to you.

4. This is usually the point where, out of offense, people leave a church that they have attended for years.

5. Pause for a second and take that notion in. We often breeze through the pages of a book and miss key moments of realization. Go back and read that sentence again.

6. That may look like (as an example) cleaning the whole house before telling that parent that you made a D on a test.

7. As you read this book, feel free to substitute the word "church" with the word "family" at any time, as many issues start in the home.

8. By "leadership," I am referring to anyone who occupies a position of leadership within the church.

BREANNA M. SPRIGGS, LPC-S

2

Ethics: What's Okay/Not Okay

Being safe is not just an emotional concept that only includes making the people around you feel a certain way or not feel a certain way. Being safe requires us to have very clear principles in place that hold us accountable to clear and concrete boundaries. As a counselor, I am connected to a licensing board that holds me accountable to a very clear set of ethics, and there is also a clear set of consequences that I receive when I operate outside of these ethics. Unfortunately, within the church this is not always so. Technically, how we conduct ourselves as Christians should be governed by the Bible, but we have seen the Bible abused and used to support our unhealthy patterns too often.

This chapter will cover three basic ethics that, if implemented, will increase our ability to be safe and to be churches that heal more than we hurt. These are not foreign concepts; you may very well know and understand their importance. However, if we think back to our barriers, our mistake has been not prioritizing and being intentional about implementing what we know keeps us safe. Those three ethics are confidentiality, integrity-driven practices, and the concept of two or three witnesses.

One of the indictments that has been brought against the church has been that "everyone is in everyone's business." This is basically a way to say that we have not faithfully adhered to the ethical standard of maintaining the confidentiality of others and that we have allowed gossip to permeate our cultures. Confidentiality (not secrecy) is the first step to becoming a safe place. When people can come into the church and know that their story and their current condition are safe with the people with whom they entrust themselves to be in community, then authenticity becomes the norm and fear can be defeated. As I stated earlier, we know this. We are well aware of the safety that confidentiality provides. Our error is that many of us have only used confidentiality when it directly benefits the reputation of the greater establishment. When the release of information stands to hurt the institution of the church, we have not failed to employ confidentiality. However, if we are to be truthful, we have not been as careful when our release of information only stands to hurt one person or one family. This notion alone makes us extremely unsafe.

Confidentiality must become the standard. We must know that when a sister or brother comes to us, their situation does not become stock material for the next dinner-table discussion or an example in the next sermon. Imagine confiding in a minister about something that recently happened within your marriage and then coming to church, only to hear that someone else had been made privy to your situation. I would imagine that you would feel exposed, vulnerable, unsafe, and maybe even guilty, depending upon how they shared your story. We must also remember that even the testimonies of others are not ours to tell. I understand church culture, so I would venture to say that if you would like to use someone's story or testimony as an example, ask permission before you do.

In the counseling world, it is understood that a person may never truly open up without the promise of confidentiality. With this in mind, counselors maintain a strict policy of confidentiality, require the client to give written permission when information is released, and at the beginning of establishing the therapeutic relationship we explain all scenarios that would require us to break confidentiality without the client's permission. Adopting these practices in ministry would be a building block in becoming safer as a church. Let's explore what that might look like.

First, pastors and church leadership should commit to confidentiality. When members of the church come to you with their personal affairs, minister to them and keep the information shared confidential. If there is a situation where (for example) you would like to submit that information or some form of it[9] as a prayer request, ask permission. In fact, I encourage you to offer everyone the option to submit prayer requests in writing, as opposed to everyone only speaking their personal prayer request aloud in front of the entire prayer group. If we are not careful, our methods of taking prayer requests can become a hub for gossip. A simple prayer request given on behalf of someone else may turn into story time and then graduate into gossip if we are not careful of how we share the request.

In the case of children and teens, they should be informed that their parents can be given any information about them or what they express in different group/ministry settings that they request or that causes concern. However, when youth groups, etc., are formed, hold meetings to coordinate with parents about the types of discussions that will take place and the protocols that are in place when a child or teen expresses something that is a cause for concern. Also, define what those causes for concern are for both the parents and the children. Children and teens should feel safe expressing themselves openly in group ministry settings, and parents should feel safe sending their children and teens into these settings without the fear that a youth group leader will not inform them of serious matters that are happening with their child. Informing parents while maintaining rapport with a teen can be tricky business. What helps is to be honest and upfront with the young person about your concern and the fact that their parent should be informed. Ask them if they would like to share that information with their parent, if they would like you to share it, or if they would like for all three of you to come together and talk about it. The same protocol could be used if you are not in leadership and if you ever, under any circumstances, become privy to concerning information about another child or teen in your church.

Finally, in the area of confidentiality, we must know the circumstances under which confidentiality is no longer safe. In the counseling world, we "break confidentiality" when a person expresses information that confirms that they are at risk of being a danger to themselves or someone else. This may include suicidal plans, homicidal plans, and reports of abuse. This standard should be implemented in the church as nonnegotiable circumstances under which confidentiality may acceptably be broken.

Outside of that, I understand that in a church setting there are many situations where breaking confidentiality could be necessary in order to guide a person to the proper level of support within the community. It is important that you understand that it can be difficult to restore the rapport or relationship that you once had with someone after breaking their confidentiality. You must be sure that breaking confidentiality, in that instance, is more important than keeping the relationship or rapport before you decide to do so.

Exercise

What are some other situations that you believe would be cause for "breaking confidentiality"?

1. _____

2. _____

3. _____

Whatever you may have identified, be sure that you are willing to inform those that you mentor, minister to or lead groups with that if such information comes up, you may be inclined to break their confidentiality. The truth is that there are situations where you think that breaking confidentiality is necessary, and it may not be. However, in order to account for those differences, inform the person who is trusting you with their information of these standards and ask permission before sharing their information. It is as simple as, "I think that this information should be shared with Pastor So-and-So. Would it be okay with you if I do so?"

Our second branch of ethics that will help us become a safer church is the employment of integrity-driven practices. At a glance this may sound general, but it is a rule of thumb. If we measure everything that we do by the level of integrity we display, then we stand to increase our measure of safety. As a church and as members of the body of Christ, we should display integrity in how we interact with each other, how we operate within our relationships and family, how we do business, and the public images that we portray both in person and on social media. There is no way that a person will feel safe in our church after they have witnessed us cut corners in our business practices. People will not feel safe in our church after being attacked by one of our ministers on Facebook for doctrinal or political differences. People will not feel safe in our church after being inappropriately flirted with by a leader in our church. Integrity matters.

As a church, we should have integrity in how we conduct a service. Something so simple as starting on time communicates to members that their time is valued. Offering is a necessary part of church services, and giving is biblical; however, the way in which we ask for money and use the money that we collect should be done with integrity. Being transparent with members about where their money goes is important and shows integrity. Being respectful of marriages and families is important. It takes integrity to send people home and not cause people to choose between devotion to their family and devotion to the house of God. Transitioning between churches and releasing members to transition between churches should be done with integrity and not strife. Our methods of promoting and demoting[10] should be done with integrity and careful spiritual insight. There were times where people complained that the young woman who became pregnant was demoted from the choir, while the young man who fathered the child remained on the drums. Practices like these bring our integrity into question. The Bible demonstrates this when it speaks of partiality, or "respect of persons," and a false balance.

As a church, we must prioritize integrity over the systems that we have settled into over the years, and we must hold each other accountable to maintaining that integrity in all our practices. I believe that many of the scandals that have taken place in churches across the country are only a byproduct of the slow erosion of our integrity. The simple things that we said were no longer necessary or took too much time eventually ended up being the keys to the church maintaining a reputation of being a safe and upstanding place of refuge. The Bible tells us that a good name should be chosen over great riches (Proverbs 22:1). In that passage, the word "name" means reputation. We must return to valuing our reputation over our image. A good image can only attract people, but a good reputation is what will help us to connect to people.

The third ethical practice that I would like to discuss is the concept of "two or three witnesses." This concept comes from many Scriptures in the New Testament where words had to be established by two or three witnesses. There is even a Scripture that encourages a witness to be brought in when a problem could not be resolved between two individuals in the church. Why is this important to us? Because we often neglect the power that is in numbers. I remember having a male doctor when I was much younger, and there were certain procedures that he could not perform on me without a nurse being present. This was both for his safety and for mine.

As I mentioned earlier, we understand the value of this concept, because we use it in some instances and not in others. For example, we encourage members of the church to have pastors, mentors, and accountability partners, but the higher we get, the less we need them for ourselves. Here are two scenarios that the church has continually tripped over that the concept of two or three witnesses can help us: male pastors privately counseling female members. This one scenario has been the source of scandal after scandal after scandal in the church. The second scenario is the mistreatment of members by middle leadership in the name of authority.

There are two practical ways that the concept of two or three witnesses may be used to help us to avoid these scenarios as we move forward. The first way is the use of husband-and-wife teams. In the Bible, Paul raved about Priscilla and Aquila and the powerful ministry that they had together (Romans 16:3–5). In situations where an individual needs guidance or personal mentorship from someone in

BREANNA M. SPRIGGS, LPC-S

spiritual leadership, whether of the opposite sex or the same sex,[11] the involvement and—at the very least—awareness of that leader's spouse can safeguard everyone involved.

Much of the abuse and exploitation that has happened within the walls of the church have started with a simple, one-on-one meeting. Am I implying that we are incapable of having one-on-one meetings in a safe manner? No, but I am saying that we have often fallen victim to being naïve about all that we are capable of when our flesh is unchecked and unguarded.

Marriage was not given only for social reasons; it was something instituted by God as a tool to aid and support our purposes and ministries. A spouse is a great accountability partner because they see every side of us, beyond the representations that we take out into public. The use of husband-and-wife teams in ministry safeguards individuals and churches from scandal because it honors the design of God. I can hear someone now: "But Jesus wasn't married!" My answer is that Jesus literally walked around with twelve accountability partners.

However, that does bring into question single pastors and leaders. What protocols can be put into place for a single, male pastor who must often minister to the women in his church? This is where it would be wise to still utilize married couples; and as Paul instructed Titus in Titus 2:3-5 to let the older women teach the younger women. It would also be wise to interact with the women of the church in more communal spaces in order to remove what the Bible calls the appearance of evil.

Some may view this as being extreme, but we must understand that when things go awry, it is these women who are labeled as Jezebels and temptresses who plotted to take the "man of God" down; but no one asks the pastor why he was alone with the woman in his private study while his wife was at home. Integrity must find its way back into the walls of the church or we will continue to be labeled as danger zones because we refused to acknowledge the truth and change our ways.

The truth is also that not all unethical practices are sexual in nature. The church is a place that prides itself on the power that it possesses and the power that God gives to His servants. The church is made up of a lot of hierarchies, titles, and power positions—much more than the New Testament church was. With that in mind, the concept of two or three witnesses can also be used to develop a system of checks and balances by which leaders are held accountable and supported by other leaders. In the Bible, we see that Jesus sent His disciples out two by two (Mark 6:7). Another example of this in the Bible is the relationship between Paul and Peter. When Paul notices that Peter is giving the Gentiles unjust standards, he confronts him about it directly (Galatians 2:11–14). We are now living in a time where everyone is their own accountability partner, and because of this, the church has not been a safe place.

Please understand that Paul's rebuke of Peter was more to protect the Gentiles than it was about Peter. Peter was an awesome man of God and a beloved brother of Paul, but had Paul not spoken up to Peter, he would have continued to hurt the Gentiles and possibly misrepresent the very nature of Christ to them. Had Paul decided to create a united front with Peter, the kingdom of God would have lost an entire nation of people. I know that I am not alone when I say that I am just as unwilling as Paul to see this happen in today's church. This is why I am writing this book.

In this chapter, I leaned in on only three ethical principles that can be helpful to us in becoming the church that heals, but there could be many more.

Exercise

Brainstorm some ethical principles that today's church could benefit from. Hint: You may be compelled to identify some that could be specific to social media platforms, etc.

1. _____

2. _____

3. _____

Now, take a moment to conceptualize how the use of two or three witnesses could be used in your church or in the way that you personally minister to others.

_____
_____
_____
_____

Regarding husband-and-wife teams: If you are married, what are some ways that your spouse has been or could be a support to you in your ministry to others?

_____
_____
_____
_____

Chapter 2 Endnotes

9. You do not have to give all the details in order for others to understand the prayer request.

10. Another term for this is "being sat down."

11. It is important to acknowledge that same-sex attraction does exist in our churches and among church leaders so that we can avoid scandal in those areas as well.

BREANNA M. SPRIGGS, LPC-S

3

Recognizing the Need

In this chapter, we will do two things that I have not done yet in this book: unpack Scripture and have a brief psychology lesson. Those two things may not seem to correlate with each other, but you will soon see how both are necessary in recognizing the needs of others. When it involves recognizing a need, no one—and I mean no one—does that better than Jesus Christ Himself. We will particularly see this in a snapshot of Luke 19:5, the story of Zacchaeus.

The Bible is sure to inform us that Zacchaeus was a short man, but we cannot allow that to be the only thing that we remember about him. He was also a publican and a rich man. He had power within that region. He was well known and, most likely, hated because he was chief among the publicans or tax collectors. In those days, publicans were seen as thieves and traitors because they collected taxes from their fellow Jews for the Roman government. It was also common knowledge that they made some pretty hefty profits from their collections. Publicans were so hated that they were not allowed to hold public office or testify in a Jewish court. This was Zacchaeus. Of all the stories of people whose needs Jesus met in the Bible, this one was special because culturally, there was no reason for

Zacchaeus to be on Jesus's radar that day. Zacchaeus was physically short, he was rich, and he was despised by every other Jew. But in that moment, Jesus saw past all of that and heard the cry of Zacchaeus's heart. He even extended Himself and visited Zacchaeus's home. He ventured into Zacchaeus's intimate and vulnerable space and brought the salvation that Zacchaeus and his family needed.

What does this mean for us as we endeavor to become the church that heals? Well, we must sharpen our ability to see past the Cliffs-Notes of what we think we know about others in order to connect with what they truly need. We often make the mistake of judging a person's level of need only by their income. Zacchaeus was rich, but that did not stop Jesus from identifying that he still had a need. We often look to the bottom of the totem pole for neediness and miss the opportunity to minister to people from many different walks of life. I have often wondered why churches rarely set up to do ministry outreach in "good" neighborhoods the way they do in the seemingly "bad" ones. Do they not need Jesus in gated communities? Oftentimes, this is rooted in the belief that money is our primary need. Let's explore other types of needs.

In the world of psychology, there is something called Maslow's Hierarchy of Needs.[12] Abraham Maslow developed a five-tier model of human needs and proposed that the needs in the lower tier must be met before the needs in the top tier can be met. This hierarchy of needs is consistent with the Bible, when we see Jesus feeding people and not only ministering to them. In his epistle, James encourages the people of God to clothe and feed others instead of, by faith, telling them to "go in peace, be warmed and filled" (James 2:15–16) without actually providing those needs.

Self-actualization
desire to become the most that one can be

Esteem
respect, self-esteem, status, recognition, strength, freedom

Love and belonging
friendship, intimacy, family, sense of connection

Safety needs
personal security, employment, resources, health, property

Physiological needs
air, water, food, shelter, sleep, clothing, reproduction

Maslow's hierarchy of needs

At the bottom of the pyramid, we see the physiological needs of air, water, food, shelter, clothing, etc. These needs progress into safety needs, which are personal security, employment, resources, health and property. (It's important to reinforce here the importance of our churches being safe places. The church will not be able to meet any other need until we solidify our reputation to the world as a safe place.) The next level of need is love and belonging, followed by esteem, which is topped by self-actualization.

From what I have observed, the church has been a great place where people's need for esteem and self-actualization can be satisfied. When a person's primary need is esteem, for example, they can integrate into the church, gain a title (let's say the title of prophet), and swim in the amount of respect and esteem that they will gain just from being called "prophet." On the other hand, what if my primary need is shelter, clothing, employment, or actual love? It is important for the church to become a place where these needs can be met or where people can be easily connected to places that can meet these needs.

To do this, we must first have a practical way of identifying what an individual or family's primary need may be. Oftentimes in the church setting we rely a little too heavily on two things: what God tells us and what the person tells us. The truth is that this may not happen in every case. How realistic is it for us to expect God to tell us the need of every single person we encounter in the church? How realistic is it for us to expect those individuals to feel comfortable enough to verbalize those needs? It is not realistic at all! God will not tell you these things every time because He requires us to reach out to others. He is not going to let us off the hook by prophetically giving us knowledge that excuses us from reaching out to others in our community. Also, if we expect people to ask for help every time they have a need, then we must be willing to do the work to create the type of atmosphere that encourages honesty and vulnerability.

There are three simple and practical ways to remain connected to the needs of those within your church community or family. These three ways are to ask, debrief, and observe. The simplest way to connect to the needs of those around you is to ask. Consistently check in with others about what needs they may currently have. One way to do this, which I rarely see churches do, is through surveys. Develop a survey or a poll that will allow those in your church to identify the needs they have and to give their thoughts about how well your church is meeting those needs. Never make assumptions about what the people in your church community need or assume that everyone within your church community has the same needs. Ask the various departments of the church if they have everything they need to execute the job that they are there to do. For example, in music ministry, musicians need drumsticks, batteries, strings, extension cords, and surge protectors. Assuming that every musician has the means to buy these things for themselves would be a misstep, because often they do not. A simple offer by the church to help with purchasing these essentials would go a long way in helping them to feel valued.

The next way to connect to the needs of those within your church community or family is to debrief after major or significant events. Sometimes things happen within communities and churches, and we never stop to simply debrief everyone about what happened and assess how they may have been affected as a whole. When a prominent deacon in your church dies, for example, be careful not to just perform the funeral, send flowers to the family, place someone in his stead, and move on. Instead, pause. Bring the church, or at least the leaders who labored alongside him, together and talk about how his death may have affected everyone and what that may mean for how everyone moves forward. When a storm hits the town that your church is in, make sure to debrief and assess what the members of your church need to repair their homes or to replace food that was spoiled in a power outage. Ask how the church can help. Help can be something as simple as having a group of members cook and offer free meals from the church kitchen every night for a week. The church can be a major resource—it just requires us to take the time to assess and create a formal platform for others to share what their needs are.

The third and last way is to observe. This will require us to be attentive and sensitive to the changes that we see in others. One of the biggest mistakes we can make is to notice something and, based on what we notice, not move. We all know the story in the Bible of the good Samaritan (Luke 10:29–37). The interesting part of the story is that before the man was helped by the Samaritan, he was passed over by both a priest and a Levite. Who knows why these individuals did not stop! Maybe they were in a rush or afraid to endanger themselves; but they both saw the need. We all see the needs around us every day. The key to the church becoming a safe place is to begin holding ourselves accountable, to allow compassion to move us toward the needs that we notice and not away from them.

We also assume that there will be another person who may meet the need and another chance to meet the need. That just is not always the case. If left up to the priest and the Levite, the man on his journey to Jericho would have died that day. Instead, there was one Samaritan, who had the time, the resources, and the compassion to see that this man was restored to a healed and safe place. This sounds familiar. In Ezekiel 16:6, God speaks to His people and reminds them that when no one had compassion upon them—us—He did. He saw us "polluted in thine own blood," just as the man who was journeying to Jericho was; and He covered us, washed us, and anointed us with oil, just as the Samaritan did for that man. How much more should we want to give that experience to someone else?

We often proclaim that we are the hands and feet of Jesus, but His hands did way more reaching than ours have been doing. His feet detoured from His scheduled path much more often than ours do. Our busy schedules and airtight programs have stifled our sensitivity to the Spirit. Simple things, such as stopping or prolonging a church service to pray with someone or taking the collection plate and giving it to the family whose home burned down earlier that week, will change the game and cause us to reflect the image that Christ has always wanted us to illuminate to the world. Being the hands and feet of Jesus may start with simply making time that we do not always think we have.

Exercises

What are some ways that you could challenge yourself to be more aware and sensitive to the needs of others within your family or church community?

_____

_____

_____

Develop a five–question survey that could be used for the members of your church or department if you are a ministry leader or that could be used for your family. Think of what you would like to know about the needs of the people you serve.

1. _____
2. _____
3. _____
4. _____
5. _____

Five Basic Answers to a Need

Helping to meet someone's needs is not as complicated as we think it could be at times. Oftentimes the simplest gesture can have the greatest impact. There are five basic answers to the question of what could be helpful to a person in need. When faced with someone who has a need, these five answers will give you a reference for where to begin, when reaching out to that person.

The first answer that may be considered is resources. When a person presents with a need that is clear, concrete, and specific, it would be helpful to be able to point them in the direction of a resource. A major barrier that churches and leaders in the church face is that we often have a limited knowledge of available resources. Of course, it would be difficult for everyone to have detailed knowledge of every resource in their community; but it would not be difficult for every church to have a list or directory of resources. My challenge to church leaders is to come together and develop a directory of community resources that can be consistently updated and made available to members.

This is also where members of the church could be recognized for the things they do outside of the church. You may have a deacon who is a mechanic: include him in the directory. Use this as an opportunity to highlight members of the church who have businesses, talents, and gifts that could be a help to other members. Everything from counseling agencies to daycares could be included in the directory, and then what had seemed impossible to find is now at everyone's fingertips.

Exercise

Take a moment to consider what types of resources your church's directory could include, and list them below.

_____

_____

_____

The next answer to a need that you may be presented with is support. Support can be momentary or ongoing. Momentary support may look like simply sitting with someone and letting them talk a problem through. It could be a hug, buying Girl Scout cookies, or accepting an invitation and then showing up to their event. Support has a lot to do with showing up for someone in a moment when it is needed the most. Oftentimes, in the church, we can have so many events that showing up can become tiresome. At times when you cannot show up physically, you can show your support by donating to someone's cause or sending love through a card. There are so many ways to show your support, and every one of them can send a strong message of love to those around you.

Some individuals may need ongoing support. In cases like this, it is important for you to know and express to the person whether you have the capacity or time to provide it. If you do not, simply point them in the direction of someone who does. This is also a good time to know the different groups and ministries that have been established within the church; you will then be able to refer a person to the leader of the women's ministry, men's ministry, singles' ministry, recovery ministry, etc.[13]

Exercises

Think back to a time when someone reached out to you for support. How did you support them? Is there anything that you would do differently?

_____

_____

_____

What are three groups or ministries in your church that can be a good support to members? If there are fewer than three, brainstorm what groups are needed that could be helpful to members.

1. _____
2. _____
3. _____

The next possible answer to needs that show up in the church is guidance/Scripture. Within the walls of the church, so many people are looking for answers, guidance, and wisdom about so many things in their lives. For the leaders in ministry, it is so important for you to have a solid understanding of what Scripture says about how to approach life, because many people in church are searching for that information. In his first letter, Peter encourages the people of God to "be ready always to give an answer to every man that asketh you a reason of the hope that is in you" (1 Peter 3:15). Does this mean that you should know everything? No, but it does imply that you should know your "why" and, in many cases, the church's "why"— and have the Scriptures to back it up.

Most people come into the church for guidance in both their natural and spiritual lives. The church should house leaders who have the wisdom, knowledge, and experience to be able to give guidance without turning it into control. This can be as simple as taking someone to the Scriptures for an answer, encouraging that person to sit with their question,[14] or giving your testimony of overcoming a similar experience. Under the umbrella of guidance, a person may need mentorship. Note that mentorship should not always come with a price, but it should always come with boundaries.

Making yourself available to someone as they grow in their relationship with God and others is a necessary part of the overall growth of the body of Christ. This is literally how impartation happens. With that being said, we should be careful not to exploit others by, for example, charging hundreds and thousands of dollars for "four sessions of mentorship toward your prophetic call!" In cases like this, we are literally putting a price on something that God (and, often, other people) freely gave to us. Such practices are exploitative and diminish the overall safety of the church. That is not to say that the time, skill, and knowledge that you possess are not valuable, or that imparting/mentoring does not require boundaries,[15] because it does. While mentoring in other areas of life, such as career mentoring, definitely comes with a price, the church and its leaders, on the other hand, must be careful about charging money for mentoring because we have misrepresented ourselves on many occasions by placing a price on the wrong things. One of those things is our next answer to a need: prayer.

Prayer, deliverance, and spiritual gifts are to be freely given. Practices like money lines[16] are nothing more than exploiting the vulnerability of God's people. People come to services, revivals, and conferences hungry for a word from God or a special prayer and are willing to give anything to the person who has it. Exploiting this vulnerability has made the church and its leaders unsafe. We should also be careful about reminding people of how we prayed for them when we ask for offerings. Such reminders are a much more subtle form of exploitation that can also be manipulative in nature.

Prayer meets needs. Many of us are where we are because of it. Oftentimes, when you have nothing else to offer someone, prayer is a safe go-to because it points them in the right direction: upward. It is important that we are willing and flexible to offer prayer to others, even when the setting does not match. Altar call should not be something that "opens and closes," because heaven is always open. Also, for those reading this book who may not feel spiritually equipped to pray with[17] someone: remember that prayer is more about the heart that prays it than the spiritual rank of the person. A simple cry for help to the One who can do anything goes a long way. Prayer does not have to be this long, elaborate, eloquent production. It is no more than simply joining faith with another believer and sending a petition to heaven.

Exercise

This week, challenge yourself to offer prayer to someone who needs it. You may be inclined to start within your own home. Start with your child, who may have a big test coming at school. Start with your neighbor, whose son is overseas serving the country. Start with the choir director, who complains of a headache. Prayer may be just the thing that a person needs.

The next and final answer to a need could be a conversation. I will go more in depth about listening in the chapters to come, but for now it is important to discuss how powerful a conversation could be in meeting a need. Oftentimes, a person in need just simply needs to talk or be talked through an issue. One of the greatest complaints that individuals in distress state is that they have no one to talk to. Simply being that person—someone who listens—has literally kept many a person alive.

It is important not only that we, as individuals, make ourselves available for conversations with others but also that the church creates platforms for conversations to happen. In the church, we have fallen into the habit of always having the congregation listening to one speaker teach or preach. We have neglected how valuable open forums can be. Creating a place where groups of people can just come and talk is a dynamic tool. No agenda, preset activities, lessons, sermons, etc. . . . just conversation: we need more of this both in and outside of the church. We complain about the youth, but we have no conversations with them. The same can be said about so many other groups of people. So many needs go unmet because of silence. By creating settings and atmospheres where conversations can happen, we open the doors of the church to true freedom and healing like we have never seen before.

Exercise

As we end the first section of the book, make some notes below about what you have learned about connecting. What in this section stood out to you, and what would you like to take away as you move into the next section?

_____

_____

_____

_____

_____

_____

_____

_____

_____

_____

_____

Chapter 3 Endnotes

12.   https://stock.adobe.com/uk/images/maslow-s-hierarchy-of-needs-scalable-vector-illustration/141243251?asset_id=141243251 Image by: Laplateresca "Maslow's Hierarchy of Needs"

13. Small groups are a great resource for those in the church who need ongoing support in their walks of life.

14. There are some answers that only God can give. Sometimes the best guidance is simply to be okay with not having all the answers.

15. A mentee should not monopolize your time to the point where they take away from your family and other commitments.

16. A type of prayer line in which the amount you give determines the depth of the prayer or prophecy you receive.

17. Notice that I use "with" and not "for." In some settings, the term "praying for" implies that you must lay hands on someone and have a certain spiritual rank; in others, telling someone that you'll pray for them is simply a polite way to give a solution and walk away, never to think of their situation again. Praying with someone is a simple gesture of two believers that can happen right in the moment.

SERVE

"As each has received a gift, use it to serve one another, as good stewards of God's varied grace: whoever speaks, as one who speaks oracles of God; whoever serves, as one who serves by the strength that God supplies--in order that in everything God may be glorified through Jesus Christ. To him belong glory and dominion forever and ever. Amen." 1 Peter 4: 10-11

4

Empty Cups Can't Pour

Serving is major in the eyes of God. When the disciples argued about who was the greatest among them, Jesus told them that the greatest would be the one who served. Service is the vehicle for healing. Jesus served everyone He encountered and changed lives. Two aspects of Jesus were critical to how he served: the fullness of God that dwelled in Him[18] and the fact that Jesus often went away to refill.[19] Jesus—God in the flesh—went away to recover, to grieve, to pray, and, yes, to sleep. This implies that even though He was filled with the fullness of God, Jesus was still aware of His humanity and its limited capacity. Therefore, we, as the modern-day body of Christ, should be aware of our capacity as well.

Pouring from an empty cup can be dangerous because when we are empty, we go through the motions of serving, but those whom we are serving do not actually receive anything of substance from us. We must be willing to ask ourselves three questions to evaluate whether we are in a good place to serve:

- Do I have the capacity?
- Do I have the time?
- Do I have the wisdom/knowledge/training (in this area)?

Let's discuss how we may assess our own capacities. To judge whether we have the capacity, we must consider what our emotional, spiritual, mental capacities are as well as whether we have the appropriate boundaries. Having no boundaries gives us and others the false perception that we have unlimited capacity. Setting boundaries allows us to operate in the truth of what we can and cannot do. In order to establish this, we must first understand what our limitations are.

In considering whether we have sufficient emotional capacity, we must have the ability to check in with ourselves daily about how we feel. Before I proceed, I must address the long-established belief system in the body of Christ that "our feelings do not matter." This belief system is not implied; as a matter of fact, it is expressed in songs, sermons, and exhortations in churches across the world. This mindset was given to us in order to build a fortitude and strength that pushes us to continue to work and "get the job done" even when we do not feel like doing so. Although this is a great mindset to have, there are two sides to every coin. This has graduated from a mere saying that gets us through having the "don't wants" to a mindset that keeps us going through motions, even when we are dying inside.

Take a moment to consider what "not having the emotional capacity" may look like for you. It may be times when someone is talking to you about their problems, but you spend the whole time holding back tears about problems of your own. It may be after someone close to you dies. You may need a few weeks or even months to grieve, as opposed to a few days or one service. It may be during a time when your marriage is going through growing pains, and you may not feel up to planning the next marriage social at church. Your emotional capacity may be to attend one, but not to *plan* one.

The times when our spiritual capacity is low can be tricky, because it is much easier to fly under the radar during these times. It is so easy for us to get up and preach, sing, play, etc., when internally we feel miles away from God, because we can do many of those tasks in our sleep. These are times when the condition of our spirit or life is not in alignment with the spiritual values and standards that we publicly proclaim. Even though none of us are perfect, we know when our relationship with God is not in the best place. Taking time away to refill when our spiritual capacity is low is a service in and of itself. Doing so requires us to value the quality of what we spiritually impart to God's people and our own relationship with God more than we value performance and our own personal images.

Having a low mental capacity is much easier to detect. In these times, we can be forgetful, preoccupied, and much more obviously inoperative. Believe it or not, many of us will still try to serve in such a state. Consider how many times you went to church, performed your normal tasks, and went straight home afterward to bury yourself right back under your bed covers. Consider how many times you have checked out during the pastor's sermon or worship service because your mind was somewhere else. There are all signs of low mental capacity.

Times of low capacity (emotional, spiritual, or mental) require us to occupy the posture of receiving more than serving. Again, we have often praised people for giving when they themselves had needs; but we should also make sure that we encourage each other to sit and receive when it is time to refill. As a church, we can develop rotations to require those who serve in different capacities to periodically take time from serving in order to catch what those individuals may not be aware of within themselves.

I would like to take this time to bring attention to children's church workers, who are always with the children during services. Please make sure that there is a healthy rotation of personnel that allows these individuals to enjoy "big people's" church from time to time. I also want to bring attention to musicians, whose hands are always occupied during the worship service. Although playing an instrument is worship, as a musician I know that it feels so good when we get a moment to lift our hands in worship to God as well. Last, I will spotlight pastors, who preach every service. It is important that they hear the preached Word of God as well: Scripture says that faith comes by hearing. Every year, take some Sundays to simply hear the Word of God from someone else.[20]

Exercise

Take some time to consider what signs may let you know when your capacity is low. How do you know when it is time for you to refill and recover?

_____

_____

_____

_____

When considering our capacity to serve, we must also evaluate how much time we have. Serving is something that you must be able to make time for or have the capacity to do and continue doing. Oftentimes, we overcommit ourselves to things that we do not have the time to do. Before committing to serving, you must first ask yourself if you have the time and availability to do so. Truth be told, this may look different in the different times and seasons of your life. Set realistic expectations of yourself, and establish your boundaries based on these expectations. When you are single with no children, your capacity will be much different from when you are married with children. If you have children, your capacity will be much different in the summer than in middle of the school year. You must take all of this into consideration when setting your boundaries and giving your word to others.

I know what you may be thinking: "God is more important than all of those things." He most definitely is. However, we must remember that God is in all those things as well. Whose is it to say that the service we do on a Wednesday night at church means more to God than the service we do in raising our children on a Wednesday night at home? I believe that God gets the glory out of all of it. What He does not get the glory from is when we say "yes" out of a sense of obligation and then end up neglecting everything because we did not have the time to do anything. Setting healthy boundaries in our commitments to service may look like everyone being aware of and communicating their best days of availability and serving freely within those times. Otherwise, we will end up with a body of people who are physically depleted, overly extended, and frustrated, pouring out of empty cups.

It is also important that we set boundaries that allow us to adjust our availability when we are sick or tired. We often applaud people for continuing to do things despite being sick, and we downright dismiss the idea of taking a break because we are tired. Keep in mind that what we praise, we raise. By this I mean that if we praise people for serving while they are sick, we increase the likelihood that people will serve while they are sick. As a result, we also send the message to others that it is not praiseworthy for them to stay home when they are sick. As time progresses, this develops into an unspoken rule that "you cannot stay home, even when you are sick." In order to counteract this, we must intentionally promote self-care and verbalize to those who serve within our church community that it is okay to stay home or to choose not to serve when sick. The healing power of God is available to those who are sick, but it is so that God can be glorified and not to give us an excuse not to stop and take care of ourselves.

During the COVID pandemic, we saw people begin to urge people to "stay home if you are sick" because they were afraid of becoming sick themselves. However, people would still persist in going to work, to church, to the grocery store, and wherever else they needed to go. Why? Do you think it was because they did not trust the government or their own bodies? No. It was because of the same mindset that we have been operating in for centuries and generations: the mindset that our worth is attached to our work and that the minute I stop doing, my worth begins to slowly diminish.

The key to not pouring out of empty cups is to understand that we are refilled when we take the time to simply be with God and not just do for God. The story of Mary and Martha demonstrates this. While Martha chose to be busy, Mary chose to sit at Jesus's feet to receive. We must not become so involved in working for the kingdom of God that we forget to receive the kingdom of God (Mark 10:15).

When considering whether we are in a good place to serve, the next question we must ask ourselves is, "Do I have the wisdom/knowledge/training in this area?" We often find ourselves pouring from an empty cup because we lack knowledge or skill in that area. It does not disqualify us from ever serving in that area, but we need the humility to seek more knowledge and guidance in that area before we step up to serve or help others there. James 1:5 tells us that if we lack wisdom, ask God, who gives generously to all.

In this season, being a safe place will require us to value seeking God for growth in the areas where we desire to serve both before and during the times that we serve. If you are in music ministry, for example, take time to invest in perfecting your singing or playing gifts and take the time to learn the song. Value God and His people enough to go past just showing up to sing or play. If you desire to teach or preach, study the Word of God. Be careful not to stand before God's people and elaborate on your opinions. People shape their lives by the words that come from behind the pulpit, and we should not take that lightly. If you are in church administration, learn about accounting and keeping records properly. Taking the time to invest in our gifts will only add value and substance to the quality of how we serve.

One of my favorite descriptions in the Bible was of the prophet Daniel. The Bible says that the queen declared that he had an "excellent spirit" (Daniel 5:12). I believe that we, as the people of God, can carry that same excellent spirit within us because we have the Holy Spirit. I believe in the spiritual gifts and the anointing that we do not work for. I myself have seen things pour out of me that I know I could not have worked, studied, or trained enough to produce. However, even those things required me to spend time in the face of God. The gifts and calling of God are without repentance (Romans 11:28). This means that God does not take back the gifts that He bestows upon us, whether we steward them well or not. However, it is important that we do steward them well if we are to be safe. All roads still lead to safety.

When everyone who is serving at church does so from full cups, this ensures that what each person receives is healthy and from healthy places. On the flip side, if most of the people serving are depleted, tired, frustrated and ill-equipped, they are at risk of harming those whom God has placed within their care simply because they have not stopped to allow God to refill them in the areas where they are empty.

Exercise

Consider the gifts that you have. What are some ways that you can seek to grow in and perfect those gifts?

_____

_____

_____

_____

_____

_____

_____

Chapter 4 Endnotes

18. Ephesians 1:23; Colossians 1:19; and Colossians 2:9.

19. Luke 4:1, 14–15; Mark 6:30–32; Matthew 14:12–13; Luke 6:12–13; Luke 22:39–44; and Luke 5:16.

20. Preferably not at your church. Take a Sunday to go and hear another pastor preach. Visit another church, sit, and simply be a sheep for a few Sundays out of the year.

BREANNA M. SPRIGGS, LPC-S

The LEAD Model

When someone comes to us in need, the way we respond to them can be critical to how they are able to resolve and progress past the challenge they are facing at that moment. Truth be told, even with us knowing how important our responses can be to someone, there is no guarantee that we will have all the right answers at any given moment. The LEAD model is a practical way to respond to others when they approach you for help or support. The LEAD model highlights and directs our focus to what every person needs when they reach out and ask for help. The four phases of the LEAD model are to Listen, Empathize, Apply, and Direct. As we move forward, we will unpack each of these phases and explore how they will be beneficial to supporting others.

Listen

It is important that you approach serving and ministry with the understanding that listening is a major key to being effective. Listening builds trust, establishes safety, and gives us, as leaders, a sense of clarity about what the person needs. Two important elements to being an effective listener is to be judgment free and simply allow the person to talk. Creating a judgment-free zone is important because it allows the person to feel safe to speak the whole truth. If a person is concerned about being judged, then they may never release everything that needs to be said. Being judgment free allows you to listen without trying to discern "what the problem really is" or what the solution may be.[21] Allowing the person to talk gives them the space to release their thoughts or feelings without interruption. We may not realize it, but one interjection can deter a person's thought process and cause them to feel uncomfortable about expressing themselves.

Being judgment free is understanding that a person may say something "wrong," may have done something wrong, or views something in "the wrong way." The priority is to listen and not to correct. Correcting too quickly teaches others that upholding the look of being right is more important than being authentically where they are and working to develop and grow into where they need to be. This is remedied by simply being an open ear and fighting the urge to fix.

You will be tempted to jump into problem-solving mode, correction mode, or teaching mode; but if you do so, you risk causing the person to feel invalidated. To avoid this, you must understand what is appropriate for the present time. The time to listen is not the time to challenge someone's perception of reality by saying or insinuating that the situation may not be what the person thinks it is. This is not the time to "rightly divide." It is the time to simply allow the person to speak. In 1 Kings 3:16–28, Solomon listened to each woman's story before he made a judgment. Solomon's willingness to allow both women's stories to be heard left space for wisdom to kick in. By not listening fully, we often overtalk the chance to hear both the cries of someone's heart and the wisdom of God echoing in our own heart.

Empathize

We may not realize it, but everything we see the Spirit of God do in the Old Testament and Jesus do in the New Testament is motivated by empathy or compassion. The Bible says that when God saw that the earth was without form and void, His Sprit moved. In so many instances in the New Testament, we see Jesus being moved with compassion toward the needs of others. This is the same empathy and compassion with which we must approach ministering to those in our church community.

Empathy is the ability to place ourselves in the shoes of others. Empathy causes us to stop and ask ourselves: What if it were me? What if that were my child? What if that were my marriage? Taking a moment to consider that and to connect with the feelings of that person immediately kills the hierarchy and places us face-to-face and heart-to-heart with the person, who sits in front of us. Empathy reminds us that what we are hearing is not only a problem to be solved but a life and experience that this person lives daily.

It is also important to recognize that empathy may be difficult for you when someone is being open with you about something that is a sin.[22] For example, it may be difficult for you to empathize with a man who is confessing an extramarital affair to you. Your instinct may be to pull him out of that sin at all costs. You may not even feel that it is possible for you to empathize with someone who is doing something so harmful. While you very well may not be able to empathize with having an extramarital affair, you may, however, be able to empathize with feeling lonely and cold in a marriage. Start there. Your connection to his experience and ability to empathize may be the key to helping him to walk out of the grip of what could ultimately cause him to lose his family. Having a glimpse into someone else's struggle should make us want to extend compassion even more.

When considering empathy, we must accept that it must be extended to everyone, regardless of who they are or what they have done. Empathy flows out of you because that is what resides in you. Empathy also flows from our understanding of how much of an impact the love of God makes when we extend it. Let's take a moment to exercise our empathy muscles.

Exercise

Imagine that you are looking at someone who is stuck in quicksand. For a second, place yourself in that person's shoes. How might you feel emotionally and physically? What might you be thinking? What might you be afraid of? Describe it below.

_____

_____

_____

_____

_____

_____

Now, take a second to consider what it took for you to insert yourself into those shoes. What did you have to think about, consider, or even envision? Did you have to think back to a time when you were in a similar situation? Did you find that you could not place yourself into those shoes at all?

Believe it or not, empathy in everyday interactions will require you to have the same intention that we used for this exercise. It may call for you to think back to a time when you may have felt how the person in front of you now feels. It may require you to not think about yourself and to think only about how difficult the circumstance may be for that person.

When expressing empathy, the goal is to connect to how the person feels as opposed to comparing or differentiating yourself from them. In other words, this would not be the best time to make it known that the situation that is troubling them would not be a problem for you. Honestly, it may not even be the best time to mention how the situation is no problem for God. Before jumping to build a person's faith, you must be able to sit with them in that moment of difficulty. Allow yourself to truly understand what that moment feels like for them from their point of view. Believe it or not, this will also give you more understanding about what the most effective solution could be. Thinking back to the example of Solomon and the two mothers: the solution came by way of Solomon's ability to connect with the emotional experience of the mother. Her desperate plea for him to preserve the life of the baby and to give the baby to the other woman told him all that he needed to know about how to resolve the problem.

Apply

The next phase in the LEAD model is to apply. This is the part of the process where you may offer or apply a certain principle or Scripture to the problem that the person is presenting to you. At this stage of the process, you may ask yourself, "What does the Word of God say about this?" Ultimately, the goal is for the principles that are in the Word of God to guide you in guiding the person.

In applying these principles, we must keep in mind that our primary use of the Word of God should be to heal. In Revelation 22:2, John describes a tree of life whose leaves were for the healing of the nations. I believe that this was no more than a representation of Jesus as the tree of life and us as His leaves. Our aim should be to use the Word to heal. There is a popular saying about not "beating others over the head with the Bible," and we all should be careful not to do this to anyone. That is not to say that the Word of God will not challenge and call a person up and out of dysfunction and into alignment with God. However, we must simply allow the Word to convict others without adding our own opinions and traditions to it. Even the most challenging parts of the Word should be used to uplift and, ultimately, guide others into the safety of the arms of Jesus.

This could also be a moment where encouragement and faith-building happen because by now, you have allowed yourself to fully connect with what the individual is feeling and they can trust how you choose to apply the Scripture to their situation. This could also be a good place to offer prayer. This phase is where you will apply everything that you know about being a safe support to others in the body of Christ; this is where the knowledge, wisdom, and strength that you possess can be passed on and imparted to that sister or brother who is in need.

Both questions and discernment are also helpful at this stage. Asking questions will help you to gain clarity about intricate parts of the situation that you may not have been able to grasp when the person initially talked to you. Questions will also give you more understanding about the most pressing need, as opposed to you making assumptions about what the person needs. However, remember to be careful about the use of questions, because there is thin line between showing concern and prying. Asking too many questions can back a person into a corner and cause them to feel the need to protect themselves and their story. In many cases, the best question that you can ask is, "How can I help?"

Spiritual discernment will be a major aid in these moments, because that inner guidance of the Spirit can also provide insight into what the person needs. I know that much of what we have explored has been practical, but the Spirit of God is, ultimately, what aids us in healing. When someone reaches out to you for support, always take the time to pray and posture yourself to hear from God about how to approach their need. Understanding that you have the help of the Holy Spirit will also keep you from becoming overwhelmed by all that is happening in the moment. You will be able to remember that the pressure is not on you to fix everything; rather, simply be led by the Spirit about where to direct this person.

Discernment will also help you to be sensitive to situations where the Apply phase of the model may need to be skipped. There will be times when a person comes to you and the most that you can do after empathizing is either nothing at all or direct them to the help that they really need. There will be times when no words, no Scriptures, no prayers can reach where that person is, but a hug can. There will be other times when all a person needs is for you to sit in the silence with them. Sensitivity is understanding when it is time to cut off all your expertise, wisdom, and scriptural knowledge, and just simply be with that person.

The core understanding you will need in these times is that God does not always need our words for Him to work (Habukkuk 2:20). When the children of Israel defeated Jericho, their instructions were to walk around the city in silence for six days. Take a moment to imagine how the guards of Jericho may have felt as they watched about six hundred thousand men silently circle the city once a day and then leave: I bet God's message was coming across to them loud and clear. When ministering to and supporting others, keep in mind that God knows how to get His message to them in ways that they can receive. Your job is to simply be present and open to how God wants to use you to reach His son or daughter.

Direct

In this phase of the model, you either give direction from your knowledge and experience or direct the person to someone who can better help them. For simple matters, you help the person to take the principles that were discovered in the application phase and identify ways to move forward with those principles in mind. This is where you encourage the person to depend on and listen to the Spirit of God that lives within them. Remember that everyone who approaches you is not a "babe in Christ." Be sensitive and keen to what the person may already know, and encourage them to lean into that.

Keep in mind that people are more likely to follow through with decisions that come from within them. With that said, it is better to support them in exploring and identifying courses of action that they are willing take, as opposed to spelling out exactly what they need to do. At the end of the conversation, you want the person to feel confident in what their next steps are and their ability to take those steps, even if those steps will be challenging.

In many of these cases, the next step will be to the next level of help. Once you have fully listened to and empathized with the person, you may conclude that you are not the one who is most equipped to help them. That is totally okay. It takes humility to listen to a problem and conclude, "I'm not the one." In these moments, your knowledge of what else is available in your church or community will be the key to pointing this person in the right direction. As a rule of thumb, if you are not sure of where to direct them, direct them to the pastor of the church.

Knowledge of the resources that are available in the church and the community is important for everyone to have, but necessary for the leaders within the church to have. It is more likely that members of the church will defer to the visible leaders within the church when there is a problem.[23] With that understanding, all leaders in the church must have a basic awareness of the ministries of the church and what those ministries do. In this case, a person will receive proper guidance from any leader they approach.

With so many different levels of need within the church, the level of resource to be recommended may also vary. The LEAD decision tree that follows will be helpful to anyone in distinguishing what level of resource to guide someone to based on the severity of the problem the person presents them with. To use the decision tree, simply answer each question; it will lead you to the best next step for the person that you are trying to help. The next step may be as serious as the police or a hospital or as simple as a ministry resource.

Again, when all else fails, refer the person or family to the pastor of the church. Ultimately, everyone in the church is in the direct care of the pastor or senior leader,[24] and in serious or questionable cases, that pastor or senior leader should be made aware of the situation. When a senior leader establishes a church, what happens under their watch and how those situations are handled is the ultimately their responsibility. Making this leader aware of a serious matter that was presented to you will help to prevent everything falling into their lap after the situation blows up.

If you are a senior leader, this is where you do not get to pass the buck. Those who lead alongside you are doing so by your delegation. You must remember that how they lead reflects who you are as a leader. If you are unwilling to step in and take the lead in difficult matters, you risk causing the other leaders in your church to feel unsupported and essentially, unsafe. Being a leader is just as much about taking responsibility as it is about taking charge. When someone is uncomfortable with involving the police in a situation that warrants doing so, you should be able to step up and do so. When someone is in need and you realize that the church does not have the means to meet that need, you should have the humility to refer the person to a place that does. As is often said, "It starts with the head." Your ability to do what is necessary to support, guide, and help those in your charge will model to both your staff and members how to support, guide, and help those in their care.

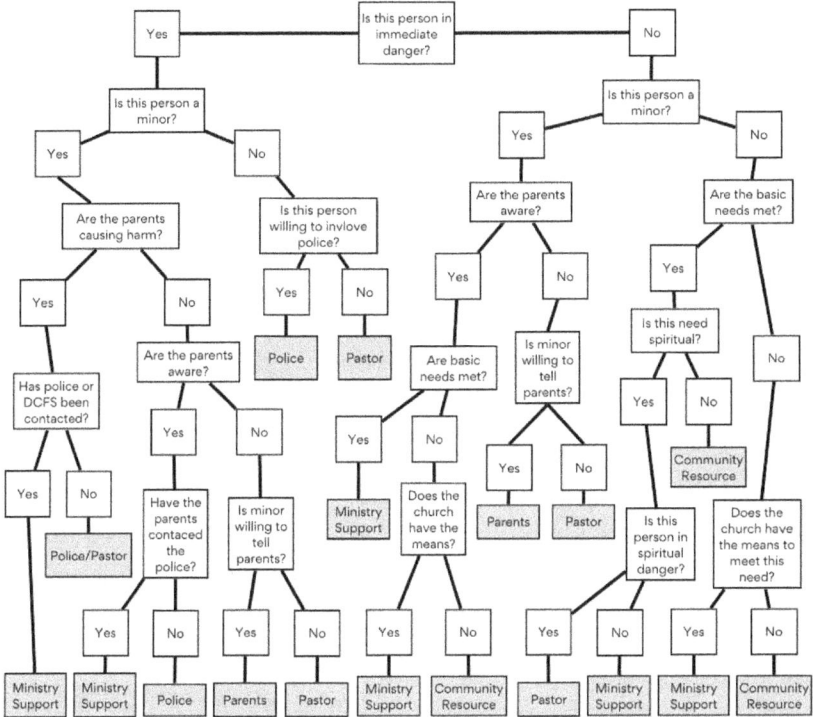

The LEAD decision tree may be used as a guide in identifying which level of support would be the most appropriate for someone who comes to you in need. Simply answer each question until you reach the final box, which suggests the support that would be best for that person based on the circumstances they communicate to you.

Developed by: Breanna M. Spriggs, LPC-S Designed by: Raghal Belloni

As you may have observed in the LEAD decision tree, the police and the Department of Children and Family Services (DCFS)[25] are among the possible avenues to which you may have to guide a person. In twenty-eight states and Guam, members of the clergy are mandated reporters.[26] Being a mandated reporter means that you are obligated by law to report any known or suspected instances of child abuse or neglect. This is important to take note of because the church must take accountability for the fact that not every instance can be handled "in-house." Our inability or outright refusal to properly report such instances is also a choice to leave families in danger and to contribute to the diminishing safety of the church. As much as you may love that member of your church, you are not equipped to remedy their habitual abuse of children. Jesus encouraged His disciples to "suffer the little children to come" (Luke 18:16). To do this, we must be willing to properly handle matters that endanger children. We will discuss more about how to do so later in this book.

Exercises

Explore how you feel about being considered a mandated reporter. How do you imagine it would feel to make a DCFS or police report on someone who attends church with you? What would be the barriers that you may experience in having to do so?

_____

_____

_____

_____

_____

_____

To senior leaders and pastors: What are some specific ways in which you could provide support to the leaders of your church in having to make difficult decisions about how to guide people who present with tough situations? Some examples of tough situations may be reporting abuse, finding out that a family is homeless, or reports of infidelity.

If you are not a senior leader or pastor: What are some specific ways that your senior leader could better support you in possibly having to make tough decisions about how to guide people who present with tough situations?

_____

_____

_____

_____

_____

_____

_____

Being safe agents of healing is not easy, because it requires us to go past complacency. In Haggai 1:4 (ESV), God through Haggai asks His people, "Is it a time for you yourselves to dwell in your paneled houses, while this house lies in ruins?"[27] He then goes on to ask them to consider their ways. The church is not physically in ruins; as a matter of fact, in many ways it has thrived more than it ever has. However, there are important aspects of what the church is supposed to be that do lie in ruins while we sit comfortably in the paneled house of complacency. In Revelation 3:17, Jesus instructs John to write to the church of Laodicea and warn them that they had been blinded by prosperity. They were blind to the areas where they were truly in need. We do not want to be Laodicea. We do not want to have a church full of people who are not healing because we are too comfortable to step out of complacency into some hard conversations and situations. Believe it or not, God has equipped all of us to do just that.

Exercise

Explore and identify ways that you can challenge yourself to step out of complacency in order to be able to minister healing to others.

_____
_____
_____
_____
_____
_____

Chapter 5 Endnotes

21. Your judgment of the situation may eventually be needed, but not at this point in the conversation.

22. This is particularly true for sins that you are disdainful of. We usually have an easier time empathizing with someone who battles with the same sin that we do.

23. Hopefully, they will all have access to the church's newly developed resource directory.

24. Your senior leader may be a bishop, apostle, priest, rabbi, board of elders, or hold a title other than that of pastor.

25. Depending on where you are from, it may be called Children Protective Services (CPS), Children, Youth and Family (CYF), Department of Children and Families (DCF), etc. Research the specific name for the child welfare department in your state.

26. Some legal articles protect your right to maintain the confidentiality of someone who is under your spiritual advisement. This may cover things that people reveal in confession as well.

27. At this time, paneled or ceiled houses alluded to a house with a decent roof. In those days, that was considered a luxury.

BREANNA M. SPRIGGS, LPC-S

6

Common Problems

Although people are unique with unique experiences, if you are a leader you can still have a basic readiness for the common problems that occur within the church. The key is to understand the general issues that may arise with that problem and to be willing to understand those aspects of the problem that are unique to the person who is in front of you. For the purposes of this book, I am going to break these common problems into three simple[28] categories: people problems, relationship problems, and personal problems.

People Problems

People problems have been common in the church since Bible days. In the Old Testament, the children of Israel were ready to stone Moses because they were thirsty (Exodus 17:2–4). In the New Testament, the Grecians murmured against the Jews for neglecting their widows in the daily service of food (Acts 6:1).[29] In a community of people who all have needs, who all have problems, and who are all still allowing the Spirit of God to process their character, there will be conflict.

Just as it was in the Bible, that conflict will often be brought to church leadership. How you address and manage conflict can make or break your church's culture. It will also play a huge role in whether the church is seen as a place of healing or hurt. Many, if not most, church-hurt stories originate with the mismanagement of conflict.[30] The argument about the church's responsibility in the conflict has also been a topic of discussion. Many often ask, "Is the church responsible for the conflicts that happen among its members?"

I will answer this question with a metaphor. Consuming alkaline water and certain foods became popular due to the understanding that there are certain environments or pH levels of the body in which cancer cannot live. Similarly, we must understand that the pH level, or environment, of your church will either be conducive to conflict or conducive to reconciliation. If conflict continues to occur and is often the reason for the hurt of those inside of the church, then we must take responsibility for first healing the environment[31] of the church. Ultimately, having a healthy way of managing the conflicts that happen in the church will contribute to creating an environment where more resolution happens than injury.

What should you do when you are presented with people problems? First and foremost, the goal should be to seek reconciliation. Although both parties may not be present, reconciliation should be the goal. Second Corinthians 5:18 tells us that God has given us the ministry of reconciliation. Our greatest purpose is to play a part in reconciling the world to God, but I also believe that we should be vessels that are used to minister reconciliation to those within the church. This means that when someone approaches you with a people problem, you will be careful not to say anything that would advance the conflict. Keep in mind that while the person is free to choose whether they will reconcile with the other person, your purpose is to give them tools for reconciliation and not fuel for continued conflict.

When a person presents a people problem to you, remain focused on the person who is in front of you. Be mindful that with the information you have, you can only understand the experience of the person who is present. Stay focused on that. When and if you give the person guidance, do so according to what is within their power. Go back to the LEAD model and support them in exploring what the best course of action may be. According to Matthew 5:24, the best course of action is to go to the brother or sister they are having conflict with and resolve the issue with them directly. As a mediator, you can encourage the person to invite the other involved party to have a conversation about the conflict at hand with you present.

First Corinthians 6:1–8 talks extensively about resolving conflicts within the church and the church leaders' ability to judge those matters. Paul discourages the Corinthians from bringing their matters before "unjust judges." An unjust judge can be anyone who examines the situation without godly wisdom. This confirms that with the Spirit of God, the leadership of the church is equipped to judge and resolve matters between members of the church and the kingdom of God at large. With this understood, where have we gone wrong? Why do people in the church not feel safe and supported with the way conflicts are resolved in the church? Why does discord so often take precedence over reconciliation within the church walls?

One possible answer could be the loss of objectivity. In the righteous judgment of matters within the church, objectivity is non-negotiable. You, as a leader, must be able to see the problem outside of the faces reporting them. You must be able to see people past their history and yet be able to consider a person's history. The fact that the person has, for example, a history of stealing does not mean that she stole something in this instance; however, if this sister has conflict with a different church member every week, that history definitely may be at the root of the issue at hand. Wisdom and the Spirit of God will help you to decipher what is relevant and irrelevant to finding a resolution. They will help you to identify the roots of many problems. Who knows: that sister in the church may be in constant conflict, because she is in the anger stage of grief, after losing a loved one. Sensitivity to the Spirit of God and a good dose of empathy will guide you to that understanding.

Note that the LEAD model can still be used with two individuals at one time. First, listen to and empathize with each of them, separately, allowing each to share their experiences, then encourage them to listen to and empathize with each other. The goal is for everyone in the church to have the skills to effectively resolve conflicts. As you continue to speak with both parties, apply the Word of God and any relevant principles to the problem and direct them to the best course of action or support. If all else fails, refer them both to the senior leader.

Exercise

What are some conflicts that commonly arise between individuals in the church? What are some ways that these conflicts can be avoided?

_____

_____

_____

_____

_____

_____

Relationship Problems

Members of the church look to the leaders of the church for guidance in their relationships, specifically marriage relationships and parent-child relationships. It is important for ministry leaders to have basic knowledge and skills for how to help those who seek support in these areas. Contrary to popular belief, for many of the common problems that people experience, you do not have to be an expert to support those in your church who need it. You simply must be guided by the Word of God, the Spirit of God, and compassion. However, in the case of even the most common and simple marriage problems, best practice would be to identify leaders who are equipped to help in this area.[32]

Hopefully, your church has ongoing support for marriages in the form of classes, small groups, or fellowships. If not, this may be a good time to consider how something like this could be developed. It could also be helpful to team older married couples up with younger married couples as mentors. In this case, the older couple would be responsible to periodically meet with and check in with the younger couple about barriers that they may be facing in engagement or early in marriage. The same model can be developed for parents and blended families. Empty nesters in the church could mentor and support young parents as they learn and experience growing pains on their parenting journey.

Sometimes married couples can present with more serious problems. This is where leaders and mentors need to be knowledgeable about resources in the community that can be more helpful to them. It is also imperative for you to know that domestic violence and abuse within marriage are not marriage counseling issues. All leaders in the church should be trained how to identify and address domestic violence cases that arise within the church.[33] Once the situation is identified, it should be reported to the senior leader so that they can address both parties appropriately. What we do not want to do is minimize the issue, due to the position or title of the person(s) involved. Because of the power that church positions have, it can often be intimidating to even consider addressing behaviors of this magnitude from someone in church leadership. The Bible even tells us not to receive an accusation against an elder without two or three witnesses (1 Timothy 5:19). This can cause a person being faced with such a problem to feel guilty and question whether addressing domestic violence would be hurtful to the family, the church, or even God.

While you are not responsible for the actions of the other leaders in the church, you *are* responsible for the safety of everyone within the church. Just having and acting on the awareness to inform the person who is being abused that they[34] have support and does not have to remain subject to that abuse can save a life. Please be aware that this may not be the best time to inform a wife in a domestic violence situation that she should be more submissive. It would also not be the best time to inform a husband who is being abused that he should be more loving. This would not even be a time to recall how God feels about divorce. These are all good marriage principles, but if abuse is happening within a relationship, it should be singled out and resolved separately from any other relationship dynamics. Once the abuse has stopped,[35] other areas of need within the relationship may be addressed.

Families of the church will also seek support for parent-child issues. In supporting parents, it is always important to consider the age and developmental stage of the child. When children are younger, problems often connect to behaviors that the parent is trying to effectively manage. As these children grow into teenagers, parents often will need support in giving their teens autonomy while also maintaining healthy boundaries and rules in the home. Again, having ongoing support for parents who are parenting children at all stages—including adult children—can be the best way to address many of the common problems that arise. As it pertains to the parent-teenager relationship, holding regular events that allow teenagers to openly express their needs and feelings to their parents in a safe environment may be helpful. Promoting open communication between parents and their teenagers is a major tool in strengthening their relationships. Parents often grow apart from their teenagers simply because the parents have such a hard time listening to them without directing or trying to control their outcomes. When parents come to you with a problem, supporting them in trusting God for the outcomes of their children and prioritizing the relationship, all while maintaining age-appropriate boundaries, would be helpful.

Many parents will also seek support in learning how to nurture their child's relationship with God. Periodically offering classes or Bible studies that give parents the skills to disciple their children and teens would benefit both the families and the church. Many churches have had to mourn the loss of the youth and their investment in the church. We can do more to help parents to preserve their teenagers by doing two things: placing more focus on giving teenagers the tools to choose a relationship with God for themselves[36] and understanding that establishing a foundation they can always return to is sometimes more effective than trying to keep them from ever going astray.[37]

In this stage of development, teenagers and young adults are more likely to go against anything they feel forced to do. However, if we disciple teenagers and young adults the same way that we do new converts, they will feel more empowered and engaged in their relationship with Christ. I always encourage parents not to think that raising their children in church will excuse them from one day needing to hear the gospel in the same way that they themselves heard it. When the gospel was presented to you, it was presented as good news and not a parental mandate with punishments attached. I must also take a moment to note the importance of living what you preach and profess in front of your children and teens. One of the best ways to promote a relationship with Christ to your children is to show them the positive effects that a relationship with Christ has had on your life. Bearing fruit in front of your children is the best witness and testimony that you can have about the power of God.

Exercises

Brainstorm: Take a minute to write down any ideas that you have about programs that could be helpful to the families of your church. Who would this program target? What information would be offered? What kinds of activities could be included?

_____
_____
_____
_____
_____
_____
_____

Think back to how you were discipled and introduced to Christ. Which aspects of that experience were effective and helpful to you? How could you utilize some of those things in how you disciple children or teenagers in your home or church?

_____
_____
_____

_____

_____

_____

_____

_____

Emotional and Spiritual Problems

Believe it or not, even with the strongest faith, many people in many churches still suffer from mental and emotional problems. Anxiety, depression, bipolar disorder, schizophrenia, trauma, addiction, etc., all exist within the walls of the church. Those who deal with more intense diagnoses, like bipolar and schizophrenia, may already be receiving formal care. Those who deal with things like anxiety, depression, grief, and past trauma may first seek care and support from those within their local church, i.e., you. According to lifewayresearch.com[38], among people who have sought treatment for help with mental illnesses, 25 percent went first to a member of the clergy. They also note that this is a higher percentage than those who have gone to psychiatrists, medical doctors, or anyone else. This shows how important it is for the church and its leaders to be equipped to handle such issues when people reach out for help.

When someone comes to you for support with emotional problems, utilizing the LEAD model can help you to avoid many of the common mistakes that tend to make those who are dealing with these problems feel less safe. The LEAD model will help you to prioritize listening and empathizing over faith-building and directing. It does not mean that you will not have the opportunity to do such things, but rather that listening and empathizing should be prioritized.

When supporting someone who is dealing with anxiety and depression, it is important that you have a clear understanding of those experiences. I often refer to anxiety as "your internal alarm system" because when we treat it as such, we are more inclined to seek out what may be endangering us emotionally. When a person is experiencing anxiety, their body[39] is usually telling them that they are emotionally unsafe. Anxiety could also be a signal that the person is operating past their emotional capacity. This may not mean that they cannot function, but it may be a signal that they cannot function any further without giving themselves some sort of care. Anxiety may also be a sign that there are unexpressed feelings fighting to be released in some way.[40] Living with unexpressed feelings is emotionally unhealthy for everyone. Feelings that are not expressed in healthy ways will eventually begin to express themselves through a person's body and its functions. Therefore, many individuals who experience anxiety will often report physical symptoms such as chest pains, a racing heartbeat, headaches, etc.

You may ask, "How in the world does the fear of speaking in public cause a person's heart to beat so fast?" Basically, the body is preparing to run for its life. When in survival mode, the brain does not know the difference between being afraid of talking to another sister in church to resolve a conflict and being chased by a tiger. In both situations, the brain is wired to prompt the same sequence of functions within the body. It is important for you to know that when someone comes to you and is experiencing these feelings, the best way for them to turn off their alarm system is to calm down. It is also important for you to know that the best way for anyone to calm down is to breathe.

In moments when someone is clearly in a wave of anxiety or panic, encourage the person to breathe. Once the person is calm, you may simply listen and empathize with what they are experiencing.

Because anxiety is so common, people function with it all of the time. The ability to just sit and support the person will make a big difference in how comfortable the person may feel about seeking further support. The goal would be to direct the person to counseling services, where they can be supported and taught the skills to manage anxiety as well as process the feelings that may be fueling feelings of anxiety. Having someone's support while seeking those services could have a positive impact on how likely the person is to follow through with the entire process of going to counseling.

Depression is also a common problem that people in the church will present with. Depression can range from a momentary low mood to suicidal ideation. It is critical that you have a sensitivity to those around you who may be experiencing this . . . often in silence. Some general signs of depression include feelings of sadness that persist over an extended period of time, the loss of interest in their normal activities, sleeping or eating more or less than usual, decreased energy levels, lack of motivation, and thoughts of death or suicide. In addition, bear in mind that a person can be fully functioning in the church[41] and still be experiencing any or all of the above-mentioned feelings. We must have the sensitivity to persist past a person's smile. This is a function of the Spirit of God within us. The Spirit of God gives us the discernment to reach out to those around us who are suffering. If we do not lean into that Spirit, then we, the church, are no different from the world that they live and exist in every day.

Special attention should be paid to those in our congregations who are grieving and have experienced recent losses. Death is sure and unavoidable, but it is also something that we are never emotionally ready for. When someone in your church experiences loss, it is important that we go beyond the traditions of bringing meals and sending flowers. Make sure that more formal resources and processes exist within the church that extend long-term care to those who are grieving. As a church, surround those individuals and families so that they know that they are not alone as they progress through what may be the worst pain of their lives. As their brothers and sisters in Christ, we are to make sure that we are there when the typical calls and visits stop. As months and years go by, someone remembering that the holidays are not easy for everyone, or that a particular family in church will not be celebrating the graduation season as planned due to the loss of a child, could be the key to helping a family make it through these difficult seasons and heal.

I also strongly encourage churches and leaders in the body of Christ to make special provisions for the care of the elderly. This includes both those who are still able to attend church and those who are not able to attend and may be in nursing homes. Older adults are at a high risk for depression and suicidal behavior. Many of the elderly experience loneliness and deep grief due to being at a time of life where death is common. Many of the elderly must live through the loss of their spouse, friends, and family members, all while living through the loss of their own independence. With the loss of independence comes the loss of mobility and access to the things that once brought them joy, such as church.

If we are to be honest, the elderly is often overlooked within the church. We may often say, "Oh, that's just Mother So-and-So." We do special events for youth, singles, married couples, children . . . but how many events are there that target those who are over fifty or over sixty-five? We so commonly ask them to minister to us until they cannot anymore; and then we downplay their knowledge because of how different the current "new generation" is. Leviticus 19:32 tells us that we should honor the elderly. Doing so will be the key to supporting them in overcoming overwhelming levels of depression, loneliness, and grief that they may be experiencing.

Suicide. A word that so many are uncomfortable with hearing and addressing. Many people, including those in the church, take this lightly. Many either accuse a person who is expressing suicidal ideation of only wanting to gain attention or jump straight to explaining to that person that suicide will land them a one-way ticket to hell. I have even heard some proclaim that they would be inclined to tell the person to "do it." I hate to say this, but because of our lack of sensitivity to this issue, many have done it. In fact, quite a few of those "many" have been pastors. Suicide does not have an age, race, religion, or any other special identifying demographics. We are all susceptible to it in our darkest moments.

The LEAD model can be used to help those who may approach you with suicidal ideations. As with every other issue, simply prioritize listening and empathizing. As long as the person is talking to you, you can be assured that they are safe. Knowing where and how to direct a person is also important. If someone is suicidal, involving or at the least informing the senior leader of the church is necessary. You can also direct the person to call 988, which is the suicide and crisis lifeline. Have handy a list of resources and phone numbers for counseling agencies and possible inpatient care facilities that the person may access. If your options are limited, then you cannot go wrong with referring or accompanying them to the local emergency room. Above all, it is imperative that you not take any threats of suicide lightly. By taking the right course of action, you could save a life and a soul.

In addition to the various emotional problems for which those in the church may seek help, many churchgoers ask for help with spiritual problems, which may include fighting to resist temptation, difficulty finding their purpose in the kingdom of God, facing barriers in spiritual growth and even questioning their faith. Individuals often seek support in growing spiritually and overcoming the barriers to that growth. We need to know how to walk alongside each other in our quests to grow spiritually. Even though spiritual problems are more "spiritual" in nature, we must still fight the temptation to skip the listening and empathizing phases of the LEAD model to hastily apply Scripture and principles, and direct a person. As mentioned earlier, as you listen to someone, be sure to give time for the wisdom of the Spirit to give you insight about how to do that.

Sometimes it is difficult to support someone who may be questioning God and their faith. Oftentimes, when someone is questioning, ministers tend to jump to the defense of the gospel. Please know that the gospel needs no defending; however, the person in front of you needs support. Asking questions is a good thing!

As fellow brothers and sisters in Christ and leaders of the church, it is important to develop an environment where a person feels safe to ask questions. The Bible tells us to be ready to give an answer with meekness and fear, that is, reverence (1 Peter 3:16). I would also encourage you to be okay to sit with a person in their questioning. Understand that some things that are clear to you may not be clear when it comes from you to someone else. For some answers, a person must wrestle with God Himself. The person may also have to see some answers play out in their life and experience. Some answers may require that they progress through grief and healing. You must have the sensitivity to know what the situation is calling for. Your job is to simply maintain a sense of openness and understanding.

When a person is experiencing a spiritual struggle or a challenge in their walk with God, having a safe person walk alongside them in the process helps. Being that person may simply look like being willing to answer the phone to be a listening ear or to offer a prayer, when you see that the person may be down. Sending a simple "How are you today?" text to someone who is having a difficult time shows that you care and are attentive to their need. It is also important to know when you must back up. There are times in all our spiritual walks that call for us to seek and commune with God for ourselves. With that understanding, there will be times when you must encourage a person to pray, seek the Lord, read the Word, and go alone to find the strength that God has for them to overcome. There is a difference between being a resource and being the source. God is the source. All the supports and resources in the church should ultimately lead those within the church to having a relationship with God that provides inner resources that they can pull from in times of trouble.[42]

Exercises

What is one way that you could offer support to someone in your church who is walking through the grief process? What discomforts might you have with reaching out to support them in this way and how could you work to overcome them?

_____

_____

_____

_____

_____

_____

It is often more difficult to hear the questions that others have about the faith, when you have not addressed the questions that about the faith that you have. Blind obedience and faith are great, but God's ear is not so high that He is not attentive to our questions. Write and explore what questions you may have had about God, the Bible or your faith. Have they been answered and settled within you? If so, how?

_____

_____

_____

_____

_____

_____

_____

Identify three resources for suicide prevention that exist in your area. (For example, Jacob Crouch Suicide Prevention Services provides suicide prevention training to the entire state of Louisiana.)

_____

_____

_____

Chapter 6 Endnotes

28. It is really not that simple, but it is a good place for us to start.

29. It's funny how both instances revolved around food. People do not play about their food.

30. This is why pastors often defer to saying, "The church didn't hurt you, the person did."

31. Or atmosphere, culture . . . whichever way you would like to conceptualize it.

32. It may help if they are or were previously married.

33. Domestic violence is a crime that is reportable to the police. However, leaders must be trained in how to support and empower the person who is experiencing the abuse to report and leave the situation safely. Hypervigilance and forcing someone to leave a domestic violence situation before they are ready can be dangerous as well.

34. It is possible for men to be abused, as well.

35. Ideally, after much counseling and the personal work of both parties.

36. We want to focus on this even more than we focus on participation in church and events.

37. Most of us find it difficult to keep ourselves from going astray.

38. www.research.lifeway.com "13 Stats on Mental Health and the Church"

39. This is often in the form of an elevated heart rate, sweaty palms, shakiness, and shortened breathing.

40.   Talking, writing, and physical activity can all be healthy ways to release emotions.

41.   In other words, they can be shouting, dancing, worshipping, singing, preaching, praying for others, etc., all while being depressed themselves.

42.   We do not want to become anyone's spiritual crutch. If some-one needs you in order to stay close to God, you may be missing the ultimate goal of discipleship, which is to point others to God.

CONSTRUCT

"And he shewed me a pure river of water of life, clear as crystal, proceeding out of the throne of God and of the Lamb.
In the midst of the street of it, and on either side of the river, was there the tree of life, which bare twelve manner of fruits, and yielded her fruit every month: and the leaves of the tree were for the healing of the nations." Revelation 22: 1-2

7

What is Your Part?

The church is nothing more than a collection of men and women of God and their families. Making any change in the church or the body of Christ starts with the willingness of each person to make small changes in how they operate. The Bible uses examples like ants, foxes, and a little leaven to illustrate how great an impact, positive or negative, small things can make. If we all focus on our individual roles, those changes will work collectively to defeat some of the church's greatest roadblocks.[43]

Many of you may be wondering about your part in addressing these roadblocks. Three things you can do that will have a major impact on the emotional safety of the church environment of the church are know the Word of God, know yourself, and seek training in and knowledge about what you do not know.

Knowing the Word of God

Knowing the Word of God is the primary step you can take to be part of making the church a more emotionally safe place. The blueprint for what God wants the church to be is laid out in His Word;

the character traits that Jesus modeled while He walked the earth are also described there. Each person can automatically become an agent of healing and emotional safety by intentionally reflecting the character traits that are described in the Beatitudes in Matthew 5, the fruit of the Spirit in Galatians 5, and the layout of love in 1 Corinthians 13:4–8.

We often describe ourselves as "man of God," "children of God," "woman of God," or "church of God." We must understand that "of God" is a big statement. Just with that description, people will begin to look for the "of God" part in everything that we say and do. When someone investigates the Word "of God," they should be able to match what they read to what they see and feel from the church, children, and men and women "of God."[44] Does this mean we should be perfect? No. However, it does mean that even when we do miss the mark, there is a mark that we know that we should be hitting, especially as it pertains to how we treat others.

Being held accountable to the principles of the Word of God means that a person walking into a church can have expectations for how they will experience most of the people in that church. Being held accountable to the principles of the Word of God means that when a person experiences us in a way other than what is described in God's Word, we do have something to apologize for. We are responsible for matching our behavior with how Scripture tells us we ought to behave. The Word removes our ability to customize and redefine "right" and "wrong" according to our personal traditions. There is no "my version of love" and "your version of love," because I Corinthians 13 clearly tells us all what love acts like.

Knowing the Word also provides a guiding system for how to approach a myriad of situations that may be encountered within the church. We often become unsafe when we begin to continually use carnal[45] methods to address problems that God gave us the remedy for in His Word. Having the navigational system of God's Word and Spirit will also help us to discern both our own needs and the needs of others. The Word of God is a grounding tool; it is our rule of thumb. Our greatest mistake is that we often neglect the use of it in our everyday lives and in our church communities.

When in doubt, learn to lean on God's Word. It is the oldest book I know that has never lost its relevance; age to age, it is still the same. Understand that God's Word is His expression to us of who He is. This is why Jesus is referred to in John 1:14 as the "Word made flesh." With that said, if we are to be the expression of who Jesus is to the world—His hands and feet—our character must mirror what the Word of God says.

Know Yourself

In order to reflect the character of Jesus and be healthier and safer for others, both inside and outside of the church, you must know yourself. You must be aware of your own capacity, capabilities, limitations and inner experience. In 2 Corinthians 13:5, Paul is encouraging the members of the Corinthian church to examine and "prove," or test, themselves. What is he asking them to test themselves in? He specifically tells them to examine whether they are in the faith. According to *Strong's Exhaustive Concordance*, the Greek word for faith in this Scripture is *pistis*[46], which means "moral conviction (of religious truth)," belief, fidelity, etc. Paul was asking the Corinthian church to examine their fidelity in how they adhere to what they believe.

While I was being trained in a certain model of therapy, my instructors constantly reminded us students that we can be creative in our approach, but we must maintain fidelity to the model. If a therapist becomes too individualized in how they operate within the model, then they will reach a point where they are no longer doing that model of therapy. It is the same for us. When we say that we are a part of the body of Christ—which is God's church in its entirety —we must maintain a fidelity to the faith that Jesus Christ and His apostles modeled for us. In order to do so, we must constantly be aware of ourselves and where we are on that path to fidelity.

To be a healthy part of the church, you must be aware of where you are not healthy and be willing to do the work to heal. If you are not aware of the areas where you still need healing, you risk doing more harm than good. Think of an athlete with a sprained ankle who continues to play in a game as if it were not sprained. How well will they play? The athlete's contribution to the game would be much different if they had given their ankle some attention.

The greatest mistake many of us often make is continuing to operate as normal without giving ourselves the care we need. Believe it or not, this is what often opens the door to unnecessary offense, conflict, and the mishandling of other people. For example, imagine that you are going through a rough time in your marriage or lost your job Friday morning, and you are a greeter who welcomes people as they come into your church for Sunday services. If you were to examine yourself, do you really think that you would have the capacity to greet everyone with the same kindness and energy that you would on any other given Sunday? The answer is no.

Consider what it would take for you to call the department leader and ask to sit out on this particular Sunday. If you are a department leader, consider how you might respond to such a call. The truth is that many people would make the call, but they would be met with a lecture about being faithful and pressing through, and the department leader would remind them that they're going through at home should not hinder them from fulfilling their obligation to serve the house of God. As a department leader, if you respond in

such a manner, you will unknowingly have just made a person feel guilty for being mindful of their limitations and honoring their need for God and the love and service of others in the body of Christ. What usually happens next is the person stands at the door out of guilt, trying their best to greet others, and when something goes awry, the frustration they are feeling about their situation (and the department leader) spills out on people who just wanted to come and safely enjoy service.

Knowing yourself is important: it will give you the courage to tell the department leader something like this: "I am not in the best condition to serve today. This Sunday, I am going to choose to care for myself so that I can have more capacity to serve on next Sunday." Truth be told, the ability of that leader to accept your plea depends on the health of that leader and of the church's culture. Unfortunately, your decision may need to be in spite of those factors. Your individual commitment to being healthy and safe for others in your church and the body of Christ will often have to deviate from the typical, accepted, and encouraged practices of those around you— not out of disobedience or rebellion but out of knowing yourself and knowing that "if I try to serve God's people at this capacity, I will be putting them at risk of harm."

Leaders know what need to be in place in order for the service to run smoothly. However, it is ultimately your responsibility to be mindful of your capacity to operate in a way that honors God and to communicate when you cannot. It is also your responsibility to make sure that you allow God to refill you throughout the week so that you are not depleted when it is time to serve on Sundays. Knowing what you need in order to be spiritually filled is a necessary part of being in position to serve.

Knowing yourself will also require you to be able to challenge any negative or faulty belief systems that you may have about God, church, and others. Many times, our own prejudices and misjudgments hinder us from fully reflecting who God wants us to be to others in the body of Christ. In order to be a person who heals more than they harm, you must be willing to examine and face how you truly feel about people of other races/cultures, sexual orientations, religions, denominations, and backgrounds. You may have to challenge past teachings that promoted hate over the love of God. You may have to dig up mindsets that you carried into the church from your time before Christ came into your life. You will need to examine and challenge belief systems and mindsets that your family of origin instilled in you.

I would also like to challenge you to consider what implicit biases you have (and we all have them). According to www.diversity.nih.gov, implicit bias is a form of bias that occurs automatically and unintentionally, and affects judgments, decisions, and behaviors. We assume that someone or a group of people possess certain characteristics according to our own biases. For instance, what comes to your mind when you read the word "Catholic"? What do you automatically assume about a person who is of the Catholic denomination? How about when you read the word "Pentecostal"? What characteristics do you automatically assume that a Pentecostal will have? If a person confesses a sin to you, does your implicit bias automatically cause you to believe that they lack love or devotion to God? If we are to be healthy members of a healthy church, then we must increase our awareness of these biases, understanding that they influence the way that we see and, ultimately, treat others.

Exercise

Take a moment to explore your implicit biases. Write down the first, or automatic, thought you have when you think of certain groups or characteristics of people.

- Baptists:_____
- Millennials: _____
- LGBTQIA+: _____
- Jehovah's Witnesses: _____
- Adulterers: _____
- CEOs: _____
- Chinese: _____
- Single mothers: _____
- Men: _____
- The elderly: _____

When you accepted Christ, you became a new creature; your behavior changed, and you were no longer defined by your past sins. However, it is also important for you to know that Christ also intends to renew your mindsets and belief systems. When those in the church speak of beliefs, they are usually referring to beliefs about things like baptism, sin, the nature of Christ, and other biblical schools of thought. God's intention is to change your beliefs about everything and everyone, including yourself. Being healthy will require you to challenge your own belief systems, come to understand that some of them are wrong, and align your beliefs and mindsets with God and what He says in His Word. We often err by wanting what both the Word and our all-knowing Uncle Jimmy says to be right. It just does not work like that. Mama does not always know best; and, respectfully, Pastor does not always have the final say if what they know or say is not aligned with the Word of God. The willingness to challenge every other voice that has attached itself to your conscience will ultimately set you up to have a clearer connection to God's voice. Knowing and challenging those voices is a major part of being a safe person in the church and body of Christ.

In addition to knowing your capacity and challenging your beliefs and mindsets, it is also important to know your capabilities and gifts. This is important because when you know the gifts that God has placed inside of you, you will connect to a church and ministries within the church that will fit those gifts. Many people in the church are serving from a place of frustration because they are serving in ways that do not utilize their gifts. Please do not get me wrong: I am not saying that every church you walk into should immediately know your gifts and place you into a position.[47] However, when you know your gifts, you will be mindful of this when volunteering to serve in different areas of the church.

Imagine volunteering to be the church's drummer when you have never played drums in your life. Your heart may be to play those drums, but your capabilities and giftedness in this area are limited. Everyone around you will place on you the same expectations and demands that they would place on any drummer, but you will be unable to meet them. Eventually, those around you will become frustrated with your inability to meet those demands, and you will be frustrated with the demands. Similar situations happen in many different areas of the church. Someone with a good heart may volunteer to work with children, but they lack the patience to deal with the full range of behaviors they may encounter among the little ones.

Another person may sign up to teach a class but struggle to make the time to properly prepare and study the material. There are those who have started churches without counting the cost and knowing how much diligence it would take to nurture both the establishment and the people.[48]

There are also times when you will find yourself operating in a position that is not in line with your gift or calling in order to meet a need or to fill a gap. You may not feel called to teach Sunday school, but you do it because there is a need for teachers. You may know that singing is not your gift, but if you did not step up to do it, no one else would. In smaller churches, the philosophy is often "all hands on deck" in order to keep the ship afloat. Many of us will experience this because God will allow it. Yes, God called you to prophesy, but He can also use your arms to swing a broom. Yes, He intends for you to be the senior leader, but He may sit you on the keyboard for some years to keep your heart connected to worship. In order to avoid frustration in these cases, seek God for knowledge of His greater purpose in having you in that position for that season. David's time in the field with the sheep was not a time of operating outside of his call to be king—it was preparation for it. You must be sensitive to the difference. There are times when God will require you to be in a position that you do not "belong" in so that He can develop His character in you. Then there will be times where you make the decision to operate outside of where God wants you to be. These times are more of a danger to yourself and those around you.

When God has gifted you to do something, He will also provide the grace, or supernatural empowerment, to carry out the task in a way that best reflects His nature. Operating outside of the grace that God has given you is risky business. We see this illustrated in the story of Samson. God graced him with supernatural strength and gave him specific instructions on how to nurture and maintain that strength. Samson did not follow God's instructions, and yet he foolishly believed that he would still be able to operate in that same strength. The shaving of Samson's hair was only a physical representation of how he had neglected the grace that God had placed upon his life. Like many of us, he saw that his locks—his grace—was gone, yet he still tried to conjure God's strength (Judges 16:20). But it was no longer there.

So many gems of wisdom lay in the story of Samson. The first one we will extract is how important it is to nurture and protect those gifts that God has graced you with in the ways that He instructs you to. Do not take the gifts of God lightly! The second gem is to understand that operating outside of what God has graced you to do or even outside of the proper timing is risky. Samson was definitely graced with strength, but due to his lack of obedience to God, he gave his own gift an expiration date. We can also say this about Saul. Saul was graced to be the king of Israel, but his disobedience caused him to be rejected by God while he was still operating as king.

We know that the gifts and callings of God are without repentance or irrevocable (Romans 11:29). This means that God does not take our gifts away because we mess up. However, what good is having a gift without the grace of God? As we see in the lives of Samson and Saul, you can be gifted and disobedient. However, the empowerment of God and access to the resources of heaven require us to both operate within our areas of giftedness and to nurture our gifts in the way that God instructs us to. One way that we nurture our gifts is to remain connected to the Spirit of God, which is our source. Understand that we can do our part and build the altar, but the fire has to come from God (1 Kings 18:32, 37–38). In this case, the fire represents the empowerment of God, and the altar represents our willingness to honor God with sacrifice, devotion, preparation, and the enhancement of our gifts through training, growth and knowledge.

Seek Knowledge, Training, and Growth

It is interesting that God required an altar before He would send fire. This represents God's desire for us to give Him something to work with. It may be our gifts, our hearts, or our seeds. God wants a prepared vessel. Acquiring the proper knowledge of and training in our gifts both prepares our vessel to receive the empowerment of God and tests our faith in Him for how He can one day expand those gifts. For example, God definitely anoints musicians, but that does not mean that they do not have to practice and make time to refine their skills, learn songs, etc. The time we invest in developing the gifts that God has blessed us with shows Him that we appreciate those gifts and desire to operate in excellence.

Something that has long hindered the body of Christ and many churches is the tendency for individuals to go forth with all fire (zeal) and no altar. In Romans 10:2, Paul comments on the fact Israel has a "zeal of God, but not according to knowledge." He goes on to explain that this has positioned them to go about to "establish their own righteousness." This simply means that without seeking the knowledge of how to operate in our gifts properly, we will default to operating in what we deem to be the right way. Our willingness to seek training in and knowledge of best practices will ultimately decrease our risk of harm to others and help us to reflect God in how we function.

Seeking training, knowledge, and growth can be as simple as searching the Scriptures on what you feel that God has called you to do. You may seek growth by connecting to someone who has been doing the task that you desire to do for a longer time than you have. It can also look like attending a conference or buying books about an area in which you would like to grow. Second Timothy 2:15 tells us to study to show ourselves approved unto God. This means that when we study and learn, it is to show God that we want to be acceptable to Him in how we act and speak on His behalf. Note that when, for example, we study for man's approval, we risk thinking either that we are entitled to man's approval because of our studies or that we will always be at the mercy of others' approval. Neither of those mindsets are healthy. Seeking God's approval alone helps us to understand that when we are pleasing to Him, God is very capable of giving us favor with man. If that favor never comes, pleasing Him has to be enough.

It is also important that you personally seek knowledge of how to be a healthier version of yourself. Healing and growing in different areas of your life will require intentionality. If you desire to minister to women, support children, empower marriages, or understand mental health, it will require you to apply yourself to learn more about those things and to seek training. If you are a deliverance minister, read more books and Scriptures on deliverance. If God has called you to teach, study the Bible and get a book on effective teaching methods. Oftentimes, we rely too much on natural giftedness and forget to invest in developing the skill of what God called us to do. It is honoring the connection between faith and works. Our knowledge will never replace the work of God's Spirit, but it will enable us to operate in the excellence of Daniel (Daniel 5:12) and the sons of Issachar (1 Chronicles 12:32).

Exercises

Explore what mindsets or belief systems you may need to challenge. Are there any prejudices that you may have about others that have hindered you from operating in love and being safe for those around you?

_____

_____

_____

_____

_____

_____

Explore what gifts or callings you might have that you could use to help the body of Christ and your local church. What Scriptures could give you more knowledge on how to function in those gifts or callings?

_____

_____

_____

_____

_____

_____

What are some telltale signs that you have reached your capacity? What are some things you might do in order to refill and replenish yourself before pouring out again?

_____

_____

_____

_____

_____

_____

What are some signs that you are operating outside of your grace and giftedness? Are you doing anything out of guilt or a sense of obligation that has caused you frustration? Can you identify a greater purpose to those tasks and access grace, or should you reconsider continuing in that position?

_____

_____

_____

_____

_____

_____

What are some ways that you can build an altar in order to pre-pare your heart and your gifts to receive the fire or empowerment of God?

_____

_____

_____

_____

_____

_____

Chapter 7 Endnotes

43. Being told that the church has roadblocks may be uncomfortable for some, but we must lean into these things and not avoid them. Many people today, out of respect, are unwilling to overlook the ways in which the church has been unsafe and harmful.

44. Not the "sacrificing animals, having two wives, eating locusts and honey" parts or even the "wearing fringes, fasting forty days, and praying with head coverings" parts . . . but the "Jesus's teachings of love" parts and the "Paul and Peter's teachings on a Christian standard of living" parts.

45. Carnal simply means "not spiritual."

46. Strong's Number: G4102

47. That would not be a safe practice on the part of the church. A church should take time to get to know you, your character, and your track record before allowing you to have free rein (spiritually or otherwise) within their church.

48. Having the call to pastor does not always equate to starting a church.

BREANNA M. SPRIGGS, LPC-S

8

The Structure of the Church
That Heals

I have laid the groundwork for the information presented in this chapter, which will be critical to moving the body of Christ forward in a healthy manner. Making changes as an individual will have an effect and move the needle on how safe the church is, but the greatest impact will come from restructuring the system. Notice how when God revived the army in Ezekiel 37, He had to attend to the condition of the bones—the structure—first. God could not call the muscles, flesh, or breath forth until He brought the bones together. In fact, He only commissioned Ezekiel to prophesy to the bones —God took responsibility for the remainder of the process. This chapter will prophesy to the bones, and you will learn strategies that you can use to restore the health of your church through addressing some of its structures. Many people have lost faith in whether these bones can live, but God knows.

This chapter may seem to target senior leaders, but everyone should invest in receiving the information presented here. Even if you are not directly responsible for implementing some of these strategies, being aware of how they can strengthen the church will help you to be on the same page with your senior leader who does implement them. This awareness could also help you make suggestions in areas where you have influence or just simply to know what to include in your prayers for the church at large. Remember that the goal is never to completely overhaul any system,[49] but simply to move the needle in the direction of health and a better reflection of Jesus's character and nature.

Address Faulty Systems and Patterns

In restructuring the bones or system of a church, we must first identify and address the faulty patterns that the system has adopted. In order to identify those patterns, we must be willing to examine every process and its purpose. Churches often settle into some processes out of sheer convenience. There are also processes that churches keep in order to honor traditions and denominational mandates. And if we are to be honest, other processes remain because they feed individual needs for validation, satisfy donors and board members, or make a particular church's image more marketable. In order to become the church that heals, the purifying fire of God's Word must try every one of these patterns, processes, and traditions (1 Corinthians 3:13).

Many churches experience common barriers to restructuring their system. The first such barrier is the presence of hierarchies and the misuse of power that often happens in churches. Before we explore what goes wrong, however, we must first acknowledge that hierarchies and power do exist within the dynamics of the church. When we deny that there is a hierarchy, we limit our ability to see its effects. Most church leaders are so invested in not portraying themselves as controlling or having power over the people that they sink into denial of the power that they do have—and end up misusing it anyway.

Leaders, you must understand that with a title comes power. This power is not something that you should deny or be ignorant of. It is something that you should always be aware of and steward well. People become vulnerable in the presence of a title. Due to the power associated with your title, some people will make life decisions based on your casual opinion. Some will be afraid to tell you "no." Others be willing to hurt others just so that you will see, like, approve of, accept, and promote them. You, as a leader, must remain aware of this reality. If you neglect to structure your church's environment in a way that addresses these tendencies, then hierarchies will develop, and your church's culture will become saturated with unhealthy patterns and competition.

Hierarchies also create a culture that pits the leadership against the congregation. The people gain a sense of power by criticizing the leadership, and the leadership uses their platform to respond to the criticism of the people. Many have used Scriptures like "touch not mine anointed" (1 Chronicles 16:22) to threaten people, and the result is a disconnect between leadership and the those whom they are called to lead. Many people have distanced themselves from the church because they see it as a place that strips away one's power to lead their own life and gives it to a pastor. Many men avoid churches because they associate following a pastor with being subservient, which conflicts with their own sense of manhood and leadership. This results in pastors on one side and the people on the other, when Jesus's purpose was to eliminate that phenomenon. One of Jesus's main purposes was to make the Father accessible to the people. For the church to be an agent of healing, it must follow this model and not allow hierarchies to mold it into an institution that God did not design it to be.

You may be asking, "How do I address this?" The best way to avoid the negative effects that can come with hierarchies is to structure church leadership in a way that reflects the Bible's instructions. It is common knowledge that offices and positions existed in the New Testament church. As a leader, it is now your responsibility to examine your use of those offices[50] and positions, and determine if it reflects the Bible's use of them. You must also examine your methods of promotion and designation. What is the process of promotion in your church? Who do you typically promote? Even if you do not recognize patterns of how promotion happens within your church, your members will. They will know whether spiritual, social, or financial factors influence promotions. Your responsibility is to structure the process as faithful to the Bible as you can, then communicate that process to the members of your church.

The possession of gifts and titles should be taught in a way that evens the playing field. In the big scheme of things, we are all brothers and sisters in Christ, and the purpose of gifts and callings is to uplift each other as such, not to indicate one's value as a human or a Christian. They are not a license to lord over others (1 Peter 5:2–3). Many have misused Scripture and used it to develop a "person with title first" culture that has proven itself harmful. Honor is a wonderful concept, but if you teach that it should only flow in one direction, honor becomes harmful.

Loyalty or faithfulness is also a great concept, depending on who you teach your members to be loyal to. We must all be faithful to God and to our personal commitments. However, when members are asked to be faithful or loyal to a particular person or organization, what exactly does that entail? In many cases, it has entailed things that have brought God more shame than glory. For example, Paul encourages the men and women of God in the church to be entreated as mothers and fathers (1 Corinthians 4:15; 1 Timothy

5:1–2; Judges 5:7). However, in the current culture, many have used spiritual mother and father relationships in ways that have further promoted competition, secrecy, misuses of power, and the exploitation of many of God's people.

Servanthood is something that we all should extend to each other in the body of Christ at all times. It never stops. The same Bible that says that you can receive a prophet's reward for receiving a prophet says that you can receive a reward for giving "a little one" a cup of cold water (Matthew 10:41–42). Jesus told the disciples that the path to elevation was to be the servant to the other disciples,[51] which He demonstrated by washing the disciples' feet. The disciples did have those moments of desiring prominence, but Jesus redirected them every time. Restoring health to the church looks like everyone being a servant and not feeling as if servanthood were beneath any of us.

In Genesis, the snake's selling point to Eve was that she would "be like God," even though God had already made her in His image (Genesis 3:5). God kicked Lucifer out of heaven because he wanted to "be like the Most High," even though he was literally heralded as the highest angel in heaven (Isaiah 14:13–14). How much more like God did he want to be? We must all guard against this same craving that can be at work in our hearts, the craving to be like God but not in His character, love and mercy—only in His power, omniscience, and grandeur. We must be careful not to want to be like the God who sits on the throne more than we want to be like the One who died on a cross in order to give everyone access to the throne. God Himself knew that it would take more than a throne to save us. He knew that we needed the cross. Keeping our desire for power in check will require all of us to stay connected to the sacrifice, humility, and love that the cross represented.

Processes associated with church membership are also areas that can open the church to harmful patterns. Depending on a particular church's culture, transitioning from one church to another can be a painful process. In some (often smaller) churches, leaving can be difficult because their congregations tend to be close-knit and expect one's membership to be long-term. People may be able to join or leave larger churches and be completely unnoticed; this is not the case in smaller churches and communities. One person or family leaving a church with less members can affect several aspects of how the entire church functions.

In the case of churches that have a hard time when members leave, the key is to have acceptance and to adjust expectations. When God sends souls to your church, remember that the timing of their season with you is in God's hands. Everyone is on a journey from this life to the next. God has stationed churches and ministries of all types on each of our individual paths to be hubs and sources of strength to us as we journey. When we despise those whom God has placed along our pathway or the fact that the next leg of someone's journey may include another church, it is hurtful to the body of Christ as a whole. We must remember that although we are not all in the same church, we are all in the same body.

When someone chooses to leave a church, we all must remember that we are still brothers and sisters in Christ. With this in mind, note that conflicts between brothers and sisters in Christ must be resolved God's way, whether you remain at the same church or not. Leaving a church without resolving the conflict only opens the door for seeds of bitterness to be planted in both those who remain and those who leave. As a healthy church, we must reflect Christ in all things, and that includes how members leave a church and how pastors release members from a church.

Senior leaders, it is important when orienting new members into your ministry that you are clear with them about your expectations for how they should leave when and if they ever leave. If you would prefer that they withdraw their membership by a letter or an in-person meeting, clearly communicate that to new members when they join. You must also know that if members feel like they cannot leave freely, they will be more likely to seek out conflict and problems with your church, in order to validate their reason for leaving.

Church members, you should honor all church protocols when transitioning your membership from one church to another. Do your due diligence in leaving your prior church gently and with honor for the part God allowed them to play on your journey from this life to the next. Leave with a sense of peace, appreciation, and gentleness. The key is to remember that you may change your membership, but your unity with each other in Christ should not change.

It is easy to recognize how leaving a church can be difficult for a person or family. However, the challenges of joining a new church are less obvious, especially when a person is not joining as a new convert. Being a new face in a new place can be a challenge because that person may have had roles in their previous church that their new church does not honor. Leaders, if you are not intentional about getting to know a person when they join your church, you risk overlooking how a person could contribute to your church, and frustration can result.

It is also important for Christians at all levels to take time to learn about the church that they are joining. You should be received as a brother or sister; but understand that having gifts does not entitle you to a position or instant elevation in that particular setting. If you already serve in ministry outside of the local church, have a conversation with the pastor about that and how it may impact your ability and availability to serve within the church.

All believers should have a heart to serve at the church to which they belong. Remember, however, that when you join a church, you must also be able to humble yourself enough to allow others to serve you. Zeal will cause many to join a church and "hit the ground running." You must be willing to sit, rest, be still and allow God to connect you with the vision of the church before jumping into action. If not, you risk projecting your vision or that of your previous church onto the new place where God has sent you. Take the time to get to know the leaders of the church, attend new-member classes, and study the church's teachings and mission statements.[52] Many conflicts happen because a person joins a church before clearly understanding that church's culture, doctrine, and mission. If you are visiting a church and have a list of "don't likes," then joining that church may not be a good idea. Before we move forward, let us pause to explore some thoughts.

Exercises

Senior leaders: What is the protocol that you would like members to follow when they are transitioning out of your church? What processes could you put in place that would help the transition to be a positive experience?

_____
_____
_____
_____
_____
_____

Members: What qualities are important to you when considering whether to join a church?

_____

_____

_____

_____

_____

Leaders: What processes do you have in place to get to know new members and orient them into your church?

_____

_____

_____

_____

_____

The last faulty pattern that I will make recommendations about is our relationship with social media. This is a new aspect of how the modern-day church functions, but if the church does not learn to navigate in this space wisely, social media can cause a lot of harm to people who are not even within the confines of its walls.

The church must restructure its relationship with social media. Social media can be a wonderful resource and platform for ministry, but it can also be a high place (2 Kings 12:2–3) where the people of God offer sacrifices to the gods of this world through self-promotion, ongoing conflicts with each other, and judging others. This use of social media, in turn, lends the church to mockery and folly, and generally misrepresents who we are in Christ. Improving our relationship with social media will expand the kingdom of God and not cause people to question it.

Exercise

What are some ways in which you or your church could utilize social media as a platform to represent the body of Christ in a positive way?

_____

_____

_____

_____

_____

_____

Teach and Train

The next step in restructuring the church to be a place of healing is to train leaders and staff in skills that enable them to be effective in addressing the hurts and issues with which members often struggle. Although the church may be spiritually equipped to handle challenges that walk through its doors, being equipped to handle emotional and mental challenges will bring us even closer to being the church that heals. Training and equipping church staff and leadership to assess and address mental and emotional challenges is another tool that will help us avoid sending people back into their lives feeling unsupported.

My first recommendation would be to train leadership and staff in Mental Health First Aid and/or Psychological First Aid. Mental Health First Aid[53] is a training course that teaches individuals how to identify, understand and respond to mental health and substance abuse issues. Psychological First Aid[54] is a training course that teaches individuals how to support individuals after they have experienced a disaster or traumatic event. The National Child Traumatic Stress Network offers a six-hour online course in both Psychological First Aid and Skills for Psychological Recovery.[55] Training in such methods will equip the church to support brothers and sisters, who are in crisis, until you are able to connect them to the necessary level of care.

I would also encourage you to seek training and knowledge about Adverse Childhood Experiences (ACEs). ACEs are potentially traumatic events that occur in childhood from the ages of infancy to seventeen. The Centers for Disease Control and Prevention (CDC) has released much information about how our ACEs, which are scored, influence the outcomes that we have in our lives. In many cases, church is a protective factor, meaning that it has the ability to mitigate those adverse childhood experiences that a person faces. You should actively seek to be aware of what the members of your church are fighting against in order to build a better life for themselves.

My next recommendation is to bring in mental health professionals to speak with church leaders regularly. Allow trained professionals to come in and properly educate your staff and leaders on how to approach the people's needs. These professionals will also have the ability to answer questions and give sound recommendations. If a problem within the church continues to resurface, ask a professional to come in and give strategy to the church leadership on how to handle that problem. Senior leaders would benefit from connecting with at least one local mental health professional. You should be able to call and consult with this person about situations that may arise within the church. If mental health professionals attend your church, you should know them and glean from their knowledge as much as you can. If your church has the resources to do so, hire a licensed mental health professional (or several) to service your staff and members; if not, connect with a local counseling agency and purchase an Employee Assistance Program (EAP) that would enable your staff to receive a certain number of counseling sessions and trainings from them at a discounted rate.

My next recommendation is to equip your leaders in becoming culturally sensitive and trauma-informed. To be culturally sensitive is to be aware and accepting of cultural differences without judgment. At any moment, someone from a different culture could walk into your church, and there should be an understanding of how to treat that individual. Be careful not to act or speak in ways that could belittle those from different cultures.

Your church can show cultural sensitivity in many ways, such as revisiting the songs that you include in worship service and having Bibles available in (for example) Spanish or braille. I saw a beautiful example of this, when I witnessed a worship leader alternate between English and Spanish verses of a worship song. Doing so, gives the members of the church feelings that all of who they are is accepted and welcomed within their space of worship. You also show cultural sensitivity by ensuring that those in leadership reflect the various cultures that are within the church (as much as possible) and being willing to discuss current events that affect members of various cultures. In recent years, racial and political tension has surfaced in a major way and these conflicts affected how many people of God felt when walking into their church communities. Although addressing these issues can be scary, it is important that we create the space for individuals of different cultures to be able to express themselves about these issues.

Taking steps to learn from your members about their culture will communicate to them that you are interested in being a safe space. Remember when God showed Peter the vision in Acts 10? He was giving Peter his own training in cultural sensitivity by connecting every culture to Himself. God told him not to call what He has cleansed common or unclean. In this one statement, He let Peter know that mislabeling the people He had cleansed was also criticizing God Himself. Treat every culture as royalty, because God created them.

To be trauma-informed is to be able to operate in a way that is sensitive and considerate of those in our midst, who experienced trauma. According to the Substance Abuse and Mental Health Services Administration (SAMHSA), a trauma-informed program or organization "realizes the widespread impact of trauma and understands potential paths for recovery; recognizes the signs and symptoms of trauma in . . . families . . . that are involved [in the program/organization]; responds by fully integrating knowledge about trauma into policies, procedures, and practices; and seeks to actively resist retraumatization."[56] Proverbs 18:10 describes the Lord as a safe place that the righteous can run to. The church is called to have this same function in the world.

Those who have been wounded, abused, and misused should be able to find a safe place of refuge in the church without the risk of being retraumatized. Being trauma-informed means that you are more sensitive to when a person's actions are a result of their past traumas. We must be able to understand that the wounded tend to strike when they feel unsafe. Trauma-informed leaders will have the grace to recognize and approach them in a way that will lead them to healing and as opposed to injuring them more than they already have been.

Being trauma-informed and sensitive may also require you to approach common practices differently. For example, in Charismatic churches it is common for a minister to place their hands on a person's stomach or other body part that is experiencing pain as they are praying for them. (The minister is usually of the same gender as the recipient.) A trauma-sensitive approach would be to ask permission and explain the practice before actually touching the person, and then be mindful of how much force or pressure is applied while praying. As powerful as altar calls are, a person who is distracted and triggered by being touched would have a difficult time connecting to the presence of God in that moment. Another potential trigger is physical contact. In the church, we love hugs! However, trauma sensitivity will prompt us to ask permission before engulfing someone in a holy embrace. A hug may be great for you and a danger to someone else. Sensitivity is key.

Ministers and those who pray with others must be mindful of the words they say when praying with someone. Please understand that although you are praying to God, the person in front of you hears what you are saying. Be mindful that what you pray over a person is influenced both by what you believe about God and by what you believe about the person. For example, imagine someone is praying with you and you hear them say, "Lord, please deliver her from all of those demons she has." Imagine what your thought process would be after hearing someone say that! Now, imagine that the person says, "Lord, remove every spirit that is not of you that is trying to come against her life and hinder her walk with you." What is your thought process after hearing that prayed into your ear? Same prayer, different level of sensitivity.

Being sensitive to trauma also includes being sensitive regarding how you address certain issues through sermons. For example, sharing opinions about who is at fault in instances of abuse[57] or how easy it should have been for a victim to report abuse from the pulpit is traumatizing and projects shame onto abuse survivors. Please understand that even though you may not know who they are, many of your members could be survivors of abuse or currently experiencing abuse. Your words from the pulpit could make the difference between someone who leaves your church feeling empowered to live or defeated and wanting to give up.

Furthermore, when someone reports that they have experienced a trauma within the church, the pulpit is not the place to address that claim or state a case. The conversation about church hurt has been disparaging because many leaders have either publicly proclaimed that it does not exist or that it is merely a common defense against correction. In doing so, they communicate that the church does not welcome conversations about hurt that has happened within its walls. However, considering the case of Eli and his two sons (1 Samuel 2:12–17), it is evident that God was not pleased with the mistreatment of His people in His house. The Bible says that the sons of Eli caused people to hate bringing their offerings to the Lord. Although it may be difficult to acknowledge, the truth is that church hurt has caused many people to hate bringing their offerings —not just of money but of the heart as well—to the church.

When people begin to express a disdain for the house and the people of God, we cannot always attribute that to the work of the enemy, that is, the devil. We owe it to God and to the people who need the church to examine ourselves and be honest about whether our practices reflect and express the love of God. Senior leaders, it is important that you take responsibility when someone under your supervision hurts others in the church. You should not shy away from addressing those individuals you placed in leadership who are harmful to God's people. Allowing someone to remain in a leadership position once you confirm that they are a danger to the members of the church is a major risk! So many people question the nature and existence of God, because they had a bad experience with someone in spiritual leadership. It is a senior leader's responsibility to ensure that the leaders you appoint are not a danger to the people in your care.

As a leader, you should be willing to disappoint the "ninety-nines" and "older brothers" in the camp in order to secure that one soul (Luke 15). The older brother looked on with contempt as the father showered his once-prodigal son with love, because he did not understand the worth of that son as his father did. Leaders, you should understand that every soul in your church is in your care. When Paul admonishes people to submit to church leadership, it is because church leadership will "watch for your souls" (Hebrews 13:17). This alludes to the fact that one role of church leadership is to keep God's people safe. A person will not submit where they are not safe. I will venture to say that if you notice a submission problem in your church, re-examine how safe you are as a leader. In the areas where you find that you or your team of leaders are not safe, seek training.

Evaluate Yourself and Seek Feedback

As Christians, we know that it is a common practice to examine ourselves. However, it takes a special kind of courage to allow others to examine or evaluate you. I have experienced and witnessed many things in many churches, but never have I walked in or out of a church and received a survey that asked for my feedback. It seems as though people are expected to be satisfied with church because God's name is on it, and if they are not, then they are viewed as the problem. Be open to feedback. Stick a satisfaction survey in the visitor's packet and allow them to tell you how they experienced your church. It will give you a new perspective from a fresh pair of eyes.

It is also important to seek feedback from your members regularly. (I recommend every six months.) A survey can tell you everything about your members' experiences, from whether they feel spiritually fed to how comfortable they feel in the church.[58] You may choose to develop your own survey or use one that another resource or website has already developed. The key is to not be afraid to ask for feedback. Asking for feedback is nothing more than another method of open communication.

One helpful feature about surveys is that they allow people to remain anonymous. Remember that your power may cause people to shy away from giving honest feedback to you directly, even if you ask them to. The ability to remain anonymous will help members to feel safe about offering their true thoughts and opinions.[59] Oftentimes, senior leaders complain about the tendency of the people to complain or go into groups to share opinions in a negative way; however, offering them that opportunity in a healthy way should decrease those tendencies. Contrary to what you may believe, there is a wealth of wisdom sitting in the pews. A survey is a great way for you to access it.

Be mindful not to lash out at the people for what they express in their survey. The survey is for you to have a way to know what your people need and how to serve them better, not a reconnaissance tool to discover who is truly for you and who is against you. You should not be defensive in how you receive feedback from surveys.[60] If anything, thank those who are willing to offer their feedback. The church is an institution that prides itself on giving the truth. As a leader, you must often give your congregation the truth about themselves. Administering a survey will be your chance to model your ability to accept truth to your congregation of members.

Understand that five hundred people can be in one church and report five hundred different experiences. Being a good church does not mean that you will never give someone a bad experience. In addition, when someone does not have a good experience, it does not mean that your church is a bad church. One bad survey does not define the entirety of your church's ability to influence lives. Do

BREANNA M. SPRIGGS, LPC-S

not allow one survey to cause you to question everything, but value each person's experience enough to consider ways to prevent them or anyone else having the same experience. Be able to distinguish between complaints that are trivial and those that compromise your church's integrity and ability to heal. "It's always too cold in here" is much different from "The loud music triggers my autistic son." You may not be able to change the music for this family,[61] but you can meet with them and provide preferred seating or access to a viewing or green room during the worship. The key is to have an open ear and to be solution focused.

Exercises

What types of trainings do you feel that your leaders and staff could benefit from? What steps could you take to provide this training to them?

_____

_____

_____

_____

In what ways could you and your leaders/staff become more trauma-informed and culturally sensitive? What are you willing to do more? What are you willing to do less?

_____

_____

_____

_____

_____

_____

What are your thoughts and feelings about offering surveys to visitors and members? What are the pros and cons that you foresee?

_____

_____

_____

_____

_____

_____

Sample Survey Questions

First-Time Visitor Survey Questions:

1. How did you hear about our church?
2. Are you currently looking for a church home?
3. On a scale of 0-10 (0-extremely unsatisfied and 10-very satisfied), how much did you enjoy our service?
4. What was most enjoyable about your first service with us?
5. Is there anything that our church could improve that would give visitors a better experience? Please tell us in the space below.
6. On a scale of 0-10 (0-very unlikely and 10-very likely), how likely are you to visit us, again?

Church Membership Survey Questions

1. How long have you been a member of our church?[62]
2. On a scale of 0-10 (0-not at all and 10-very much), how much has your family's needs been met, by attending this church?[63]
3. On a scale of 0-10 (0-not at all and 10-very much), how much have the church's teachings helped you to build a relationship with God?
4. In what areas of the church do you currently serve?
5. In what areas of the church are you currently interested in serving?
6. What would you like to see our church do more?
7. What would you like to see our church do less?
8. Do you have any praise and worship song suggestions for us?
9. Do you feel safe with the leadership of this church? Why or why not?

In the spaces provided below, take the time to create some of your own survey questions, based on the information that you would want to collect from those, who experience your ministry.

1. _____

2. _____

3. _____

Chapter 8 Endnotes

49. Unless that is what God is calling you to do in your own ministry.

50. In the Bible, the word "office" means functions and sacred duties.

51. Who themselves were all equal to each other.

52. This may be helpful to do in the visiting stage. Personally, I would want to learn everything in the new members' orientation before making the decision to join.

53. Mentalhealthfirstaid.org.

54. American Psychological Association, "Understanding Psychological First Aid: What Is Psychological First Aid?," March 2019, https://www.apa.org/practice/programs/dmhi/psychological-first-aid.

55. www.learn.nctsn.org.

56. SAMHSA, "KAP Keys Based on TIP 57: Trauma-Informed Care in Behavioral Health Services," https://store.samhsa.gov/sites/default/files/d7/priv/sma15-4420.pdf; based on *SAMHSA's Concept of Trauma and Guidance for a Trauma-Informed Approach*, HHS Publication No. (SMA) 14-4884, 2014 (Rockville, MD: Substance Abuse and Mental Health Services Administration), 9. *SAMHSA's Concept of Trauma and Guidance for a Trauma-Informed Approach* can be used to gain detailed information and recommendations on how to become more trauma-informed. It is available for purchase at https://store.samhsa.gov/product/SAMHSA-s-Concept-of-Trauma-and-Guidance-for-a-Trauma-Informed-Approach/SMA14-4884,

57. Including *cough, cough* labeling a victim as having a spirit of Jezebel, as an example.

58. You can find example questions and tips in the article titled "How to Conduct a Church Survey (+40 Essential Questions)," https://www.surveylegend.com/survey-questions/church-survey.

59. Although the surveys will be anonymous, it is important to gather demographic information so that you can see trends and understand what specific parts of the congregation are affected in different ways.

60. I just had a scary flash-forward of a pastor addressing the surveys through a sermon. I can hear it now: "You said you wanted coffee. We put it out in the lobby. I shouldn't hear any more complaints."

61. Or maybe you can, if the music volume is a constant complaint.

62. This question may be included with demographics: (age, relationship status, race, employment, etc.)

63. As you develop your own survey, you will tailor the questions and scales to fit the specific information that you would like to gather.

*Cultural sensitivity also includes making provisions to accommodate members or visitors who have disabilities. Do what is necessary to make sure that your facility is accessible to someone, who uses a wheelchair for mobility. Do you have a protocol in place for if this person would ask to be baptized? Make sure that you have access to an interpreter, who is fluent in sign language. This may also be helpful to you, if you have a thriving online ministry.

BREANNA M. SPRIGGS, LPC-S

9

When Healing Is the Focus

Revelation 13:3 is a powerful Scripture verse for quite a few reasons. The chapter opens by describing a beast's rise out of the sea with blasphemous names on its head.[64] The dragon that comes against the woman (the church) in chapter 12 gives this beast its throne, power, and authority. The third verse of chapter 13 explains how this beast has a mortal or deadly wound, but the beast heals this wound, which causes the whole earth to marvel and begin to follow him.

How did a book about the church and becoming a safe space suddenly come to be talking about beasts and deadly wounds? My answer is simple. I wanted to give you a biblical illustration of the fact that healing unlocks worship. As we see in Revelation 13:3, the enemy knows this—and we should too. When Jesus was here trying to save the world and demonstrate the love of the Father, He led with healing—and it worked. It connected Him to the people.

Many believers in the church have complained about and been critical of people's attraction to practices that do not align with the Christian faith. The reality is that people are seeking and searching. As the church, we must examine ourselves and ask if people have been able to find healing in our spaces. If the beast in Revelation 13 represents the world and all of the alternative practices that may detour people from Christ, then that means that people see the hope of healing in these practices and will continue to do so. Our responsibility, as the body of Christ, is to make sure that their searching is a part of their own journey and not because we dropped the ball when we had the chance to offer healing.

In a previous chapter, I mentioned one of my favorite Scriptures, which is Revelation 22:2. The verse describes first a "pure river of water of life, clear as crystal, proceeding out of the throne of God and of the Lamb," then a tree of life that bears fruit and whose leaves are for the healing of the nations. Ezekiel 47:6–12 gives a similar description. There, Ezekiel describes how on both sides of the river, all kinds of trees will grow whose leaves "shall not fade" and which will bring forth fresh fruit every month and "the leaf thereof [shall be] for medicine" (v. 12), or healing. I truly believe that we are the leaves that Revelation 22 describes and that we are the trees that Ezekiel 47 describes.

The river is the Spirit of God that flows from Him and into us which causes us to bear fruit and yield leaves that nourish and heal everyone we encounter ("Because the water for them flows from the sanctuary," Ezekiel 47:12 ESV). In order to do so, we must first make sure that we remain connected to the river and the tree of life so that we are able to be those leaves and produce that fruit. If healing is our primary focus, then our dependency on the river is nonnegotiable. Our first challenge has been that we often lose sight of our greater purpose, which is to heal. Our second challenge has been that we sometimes mistakenly begin to believe that we can be productive outside of our connection to the river.

In order to reconnect to our purpose, we must first prioritize our own healing. Much of the challenges faced within the church originate with an unhealed person or system. You may ask, "How can a system be unhealed?" If an unhealed person starts a church or institution out of their own hurt, then everything about how that system operates is rooted in a wound. If a person establishes a church upon anything other than Jesus, that person compromises the church's ability to heal. For example, there are churches that began with the purpose of proving doubters wrong; others emerged after a larger church split up; others began as business ventures; some were the next logical step in growing a person's individual following. Keep in mind that church planting and spreading the gospel are a good thing. However, every church's foundation must be pure and established upon Jesus Christ. Teaching about Jesus is not the same as Jesus being the church's foundation.

When Jesus is the foundation of a church, everything starts and ends with Him. Every process and every method is for Him, by Him, and reflective of Him. For a long time, we have gotten away with using the name of Jesus to advance our own agendas and build our own kingdoms. The result of that has always been the injury of vulnerable souls. That is the exact opposite of God's purpose for His church. Jesus took lashes in order to heal us. We cannot be reflective of Him if we are hurting the souls that His Spirit empowers us to heal.

Healing has to be the focus. When you consider the mission of your ministry or church, what does it include? Is it about the building that you would like to have, the countries that you would like to visit, etc., etc., etc.? Your vision should include the salvation of the people, and salvation includes healing. Many churches have been guilty of the same sin that David committed. Many churches prompt people to say a prayer, accept Jesus, and receive baptism. Then they count them and give reports on how many people the church has saved and baptized.

The first problem with this is that God is not in numbers. David took a census of God's people,[65] and when God judged him for it, he lost 70,000 of the same people that he counted (1 Chronicles 21:1, 8, 14). The success of the church does not hinge on the numbers that we rack up in baptisms and sinner's prayers. The success of the church must be evident in the fruit that people's lives begin to bear once they encounter the church. I weep for those who have recited a prayer and jumped in the baptismal, only to end the process there. Those steps are only the beginning. The church must have a vision for the healing that will take place beyond those steps.

The second problem is the fact that numbers can often be a distraction and limit the actual reach of the church. Moses led the children of Israel, an extremely large group of people, out of Egypt. Leading them was easy for him, because he only had to follow the cloud by day and the fire by night. However, *managing* the people was not as easy. Moses tried to manage the people alone, but eventually God sent Jethro, his father-in-law, to tell him to appoint seventy elders to assist him.[66] God used Jethro to show Moses that managing all of those people alone was not good for him or for the people.

When establishing the number of people that a church will accommodate, it is important for pastors, in particular, to plan according to the room capacity and the help that you have in place to manage those people. In other words, do not build a sanctuary that will house a thousand people if only you and a team of three ministers are available to minister to and walk through life and healing with them. According to the wisdom of Jethro, Moses "chose able men out of all Israel, and made them heads over the people, rulers of thousands, rulers of hundreds, rulers of fifties, and rulers of tens" (Exodus 18:25). The concept of small groups is not some trend that the church only uses to attract various age groups. Dividing large congregations into smaller groups that have a specific leader will help any church make support and leadership more accessible to the members of that church. This is necessary for true healing to take place. The church cannot heal a person to whom it lacks access. Every person in the church should have access to the direct support of some form of leadership. Exodus 18 tells us that Moses addressed the more serious matters; likewise, it is important that senior leaders be available to address the more serious matters as well. We are living in a time where it could take months for a person to have the chance to sit and talk with their pastor. If this is the case, then the numbers we are acquiring are actually working against healing and not for it.

Exercise

For this last activity, I would like you to write a mission statement or vision of the outcomes that you would like to see in the people that your church or ministry encounters. Describe your desire for how a person who walks into your church or encounters your personal ministry/outreach will feel, or what they will become, because of their encounter. Most leaders plan for how their ministry will grow but neglect to plan for how they want *people* to grow. It is the growth of the people that will mirror your effectiveness, not the growth of the actual church or ministry.

Write your thoughts below.

_____

_____

_____

_____

_____

_____

_____

_____

_____

_____

_____

In the spaces below, write what you are willing and committed to do, in order to see this mission carried out.

_____

_____

_____

_____

_____

_____

Chapter 9 Endnotes

64. This lets us know that he is with the "bad guys" and not of God.

65.   In those days, you only took a census of what belonged to you. The people belonged to God, not David.

66. Exodus 18, especially verse 18. The wisdom in this chapter is basically this book in a nutshell.

BREANNA M. SPRIGGS, LPC-S

10

Conclusion

My prayer is that this book has ignited something in your spirit. My hope is that healing will become your personal goal and will expand to be the goal for what your church or personal ministry ignites in the lives of others.

The church has yet to see the fullness of the power that we possess in Christ. However, we are flowing into a time when we will see that power. Admittedly, the road there will be challenging; it will require us to dig. When building a skyscraper, the builders do not immediately start building up. They first dig below the ground in order to create a stable foundation for that skyscraper. I would imagine that digging is a hard and grueling process.

Our willingness to endure the hard parts of becoming who God has made us, His church, to be will make the difference in our being the church that heals or the church that hurts. We must be willing to take our own version of stripes (Isaiah 53:5) so that we can be agents of healing. Jesus took physical stripes, but our stripes may be walking through the difficulty of healing our own wounds in order to be healthy enough to administer healing to someone else. If you ask me, that is a stripe worth taking. The alternative is to never allow ourselves to heal and continue to go through the motions of church with nothing substantial to offer those who are suffering.

I love the church. Church changed the whole trajectory of my life—and that was before I actually accepted Christ. My mother was a single mother who struggled to care for my younger brother and me. The church was a community that surrounded us and connected us to Christ and the purposes He had for our lives. Through the church, I gained access to my gifts and a grounding that helped me to be able to stay focused on my life goals. I would not be writing this book right now had it not been for the church. (Shout out to Lighthouse for Jesus Ministries!)

With that said, my love for the church enables me to be able to see it for what it is. My love for people and my experience in counseling enables me to see the other side of the coin. Seeing that not everyone has had the same experience with church that I had has allowed me to become a bridge, to become a person who understands the awesome power that the church has to heal and to also understand the immense power that the church has to hurt.

As I listened to and witnessed the experiences of others with the humanity of the church, I could only humble myself and accept those experiences as truth. I could not defend the church or explain those experiences away. I could only listen and allow my heart to fill with compassion. At some point in the process, God gave me words. Through this book, I have offered those words to you—not as a criticism, but as a simple spoke in the wheel that keeps the kingdom moving forward. My prayer is that you hear my voice in the endnotes and God's voice in the paragraphs.

Our Hope

" "Beloved, now are we the sons of God, and it doth not "
yet appear what we shall be: but we know that, when he
shall appear, we shall be like him; for we shall see him as
he is. And every man that hath this hope in him purifieth
himself, even as he is pure." (1 John 3:2–3)

Breanna is a licensed professional counselor supervisor (LPC-S), as well as an artist, author, musician, and woman of God. Breanna, together with her husband, also loves being involved in many facets of outreach, ministry, and service in their local church and other churches. They serve together through music, speaking, and the production of her husband's inspirational podcast, "A Mile in My Shoes." Her main goal is to use her gifts to empower others in the kingdom of God, and increase awareness of the importance of mental health and emotional safety in the church.

Breanna earned her master's degree in counselor education from the University of Louisiana at Lafayette, which sparked her desire to promote the importance of mental health awareness in the church. She began her counseling journey at The Family Tree Information, Education, and Counseling Center in Lafayette, La., where she now serves as clinical director. Around the same time, she began to grow in ministry at Lighthouse for Jesus Ministries, where she learned to serve in many capacities. As she continued to progress, she began to see counseling as much more than a career. It is her purpose. Her ultimate desire is to use every one of her gifts to fulfill that purpose, in a way that expresses the love of God to all that she encounters.

For more books and updates:

Facebook: Breanna M. Spriggs, LPC-S
Instagram: @healwithbrelpc
TikTok: @healwithbrelpc
For more inspiration:
Youtube: @amileinmyshoeswhj

www.ingramcontent.com/pod-product-compliance
Lightning Source LLC
Chambersburg PA
CBHW032055040426
42335CB00037B/722